# DESIGNING YOUR OWN CLASSICAL CURRICULUM

## Revised Edition

*A Guide to Catholic
Home Education*

Laura M. Berquist

BETHLEHEM BOOKS • IGNATIUS PRESS
WARSAW N.D.          SAN FRANCISCO

First printing 1994
Second printing 1995, Revised
Third printing August 1995

Bethlehem Books
R.R. 1 Box 137-A
Minto, ND 58261 USA

Cover design by Davin Carlson

Illustrations by Cynthia Harnett
Used with permission

**Cataloging-in-Publication Data**

Berquist, Laura M.
    Designing your own classical curriculm: a guide to Catholic
home education/Laura M. Berquist.
    p. cm.
    Includes bibliographical references.
    ISBN 1-883937-04-3
    1. Home schooling — Handbooks, manuals, etc. 2. Curriculum
planning. 3. Education — Curricula. 4. Catholic Church — Education. I. Title
LC40.B47 1995               94-79548
649'.68                 QBI94-2287

Printed in the United States of America

# Foreword

THIS SMALL BOOK IS A TREASURE for Catholic parents. It provides a guide to something they may have thought no longer existed: a way to raise their children in a Catholic culture. A culture is a natural accretion, built up over centuries out of faith expressed in the ordinary and extraordinary events of life: the love of God, scholarly reflection, the language of prayer, Sacred Scripture and sacred music, of domestic customs, memories of saints and heroes, repentant sinners and answered prayers, legends of courage and loyalty, honor and charity. Catholic culture reached its highest development within Western civilization, but in the past thirty years that culture in which most Catholics lived and which seemed to them to be simply the unchangeable *given* of life, has collapsed in a vast secularizing implosion. Catholics who were formed by this culture, and intended to transmit it to their children, have discovered that they are opposed, not only by external enemies (an opposition they expected and were prepared to meet), but also by an emerging managerial class within the Church, apparently devoted to accommodation and surrender.

In consequence, the old culture has vanished from most Catholic institutions, but it has not died. It is still alive in faithful Catholic families, not only those of aging believers who refuse to relinquish the past but also in young families who are consciously reclaiming it. These young parents recognize that their most sacred obligation to their children, after giving them life, is to educate them so that they can save their souls. They are doing what the monasteries did for Catholic culture in an earlier Dark Age — preserving it and passing it on.

*Designing Your Own Classical Curriculum* has been written for those who are schooling their children at home. Homeschooling is one of the phenomena that give striking witness to the vitality of Christian culture. In the early years of the current crisis — the late 1960's and early 1970's, scattered groups of Catholic parents tried to establish a network of academies independent of control by the Church bureaucracy, but the concurrent demands of fund-raising, administration, state regulations, insurance expenses and clashes of opinion about educational philosophy proved too much for most of them. The home schooling movement has since then largely eclipsed those efforts to build a lay-directed school system. It was initiated a few years later by parents searching for some other workable alternative to the decaying Catholic schools, much as Catholics in previous generations had inaugurated the parochial school system itself as an alternative to Protestant-dominated public schools. A few desperate Catholic parents first turned for help to the vigorous young evangelical home school programs already being developed by concerned Protestant parents. Though grateful for the example, encouragement and useful text materials provided by these Protestant pioneers, the Catholics soon grew troubled about the anti-Catholic flavor of some texts. Before long the first Catholic correspondence schools opened, and Catholic home schooling began to acquire its own identity. It has grown exponentially over the past decade.

Still, not every parent alarmed about the condition of Catholic schools has yet ventured to take up home schooling. Almost all the doubters wonder whether home education would not constitute overprotection of their children, or deprive them of essential "socialization." Some hesitate to add the role of educator to that of parent, lest the two somehow conflict. Some are daunted by their ignorance of what skills ought to be taught at each grade level; others think they could shelter their children from much of the world's corruption by teaching them at home but doubt that they could give them a really excellent college preparatory education. Still others may have been overwhelmed by the flood of paper that a correspondence curriculum entails, or may want a more flexible approach for their children. In *Designing Your Own Classical Curriculum,* Mrs. Berquist addresses such questions in ways that will not only quiet their fears about homeschooling, but fire them with eagerness to begin.

Drawing upon ten years' experience as a homeschool teacher, Laura Berquist has written a book which is not merely an argument for the virtues of such education. What it offers is an overview of the natural stages of intellectual development, informed by her understanding of the way they conform to the divisions of the classical Trivium, the first steps in a liberal education. Thus, it is not a *program* but a *method,* perfectly adaptable to the needs of every child. As the child progresses through this kind of education, the subject matter grows more difficult but the method remains constant. At each level, Mrs. Berquist provides specific practical information about appropriate materials, essential facts and even discussion questions. But her most important contribution is the understanding that education has to do with teaching the child how to think, providing him with the tools for independent analysis and learning, not simply requiring him to accumulate a mountain of facts.

When the idea of homeschooling was first presented to me twenty-five years ago, it sounded like a manifestation of romantic counter-culturalism, admirable in its daring but probably imprudent and certainly illegal. As the disintegration of American society proceeded, parental pressure forced its legalization, and I came to see that it was absolutely essential that Christians become counter-cultural. Homeschooling then seemed to be an important defense from the growing evils in the world. What I did not understand until I saw its fruits in the lives of my own grandchildren was that it is a superior kind of education, so compatible with the healthy formation of the child's character and intellect, so reinforcing of virtue, and fostering such respect between parents and children, that I conclude it must be what God has always intended.

The homeschooled child escapes the common agonies that go by the name of "socialization"— the petty cruelties of the playground, the scalding classroom snickers at his mistakes, his infirmities or even mere differences. At home, he is taught by those who love him and know him best, who know the weaknesses he needs to overcome and the strengths he might be too shy to display in public, and whose deepest desire is for him to become all he is capable of becoming, both in his intellectual and his spiritual development, so that he will become a saint. Adolescence is more manageable in a home setting where there is no appeal beyond the parents, than in the classroom milieu, where the child newly testing his limits is abetted by an army of rebels. Homeschooled children retain their appealing innocence long after their contemporaries at the local junior high have been turned into precocious, and often foul-mouthed, cynics. One of the most striking qualities of homeschooled families is their marvelous harmony, their obvious delight in their younger brother and sisters.

An appetite for achievement is built into human nature. What men and women seek is not a life of easy luxury but a lifework deserving the expenditure of all their gifts. I believe this book can help Catholic parents — especially mothers — to find that kind of joy in the work of leading their children to God within the shelter of a living Catholic culture.

Donna Steichen
Author of *Ungodly Rage*
September 9, 1994

# Acknowledgments

Many people have contributed to this book. My children come to mind first of all. Margaret, Theresa, John, Rachel, James and Richard, thank you for your patience and cooperation. Sarah Kaiser, Maria Kaiser, Austin Ferrier, Katy Finley, Rosie Finley, Andrew DeSilva and Thomas O'Reilly have been delightful guinea pigs, helping me arrive at the curriculum here displayed. Thank you.

There are others who have more than earned my gratitude. My husband, Mark, my most valuable ally, has helped and encouraged me, proofread my material and made excellent suggestions. My mother, Donna Steichen, has made this her project as well as mine. I could not have done it without her help. My father Roy and sister Peggy have reassured me when I needed it and made suggestions that were constructive.

Mike Paietta has made most valuable suggestions for needed clarifications and his concern for this project is much appreciated.

Kathy Ferrier is responsible for many of the lists and study guides in this book, and her invaluable suggestions have helped me raise my children. God bless you, Kathy.

Laura Berquist

# Table of Contents

# Designing Your Own K-12 Classical Curriculum

WHEN I BEGAN HOMESCHOOLING nine years ago, I read many "how to" books and articles. One of the articles was "The Lost Tools of Learning" by Dorothy Sayers.[1] It was very impressive.

The most impressive of the many things Miss Sayers said was that the goal of education should be to teach children how to think; we want them to learn the art of learning. Then they will be equipped for life; whether or not they learn all the subjects possible in school, they will be able to learn any subject when it becomes necessary or desirable, IF they know how to learn.

In fact, she goes on to say, learning subjects in school is of very secondary importance. What matters is the method of learning. Miss Sayers then directs our attention to the Trivium and Quadrivium of a classical education.

When I read this I agreed immediately and wholeheartedly with what she said about learning the art of learning. But I wasn't clear enough about teaching or the development of children to understand how the method of the Trivium should fit into my curriculum. I set

[1] For resources mentioned only in this section, please see the end of this introduction. Sources for items followed by a number in parentheses may be found at the back of the book under the suppliers list. These resources will be discussed in greater depth in the following sections.

aside, you might say "lost," the "Lost Tools of Learning," and proceeded to experiment on my six children, particularly my oldest child, and the children of some (rash) friends and neighbors. You will be relieved to know that my eldest child, at any rate, has survived, finished 12th grade and will be attending Thomas Aquinas College in the fall!

My experiments were surprisingly fruitful. I began to write various grade level curricula and share them with friends. Eventually I was asked to give conference talks to help others design their own curricula.

While preparing for those talks I took out "The Lost Tools of Learning" and discovered that the particular advice of Miss Sayers with respect to the Trivium of the classical curriculum was exactly what I had stumbled on by trial and error! What she suggests from an understanding of medieval education I came to by using what worked.

In this book I hope to introduce you to a method that will help you construct your own classical curriculum, a curriculum which will teach your children how to think and not just accumulate facts. It will not be something you accomplish all at once, but will guide you in incorporating different skills and courses at appropriate ages. The method first involves thinking clearly and in some detail about what you want to achieve in the education of your children.

The first step in constructing your curriculum is to do some background reading. There are a number of books available that will help you clarify what you want to achieve educationally in your homeschool. "The Lost Tools of Learning" should certainly be read. *For the Children's Sake,* by Susan Schaeffer Macaulay, is very good. I recommend it highly to all parents, not only to homeschoolers. It presents a view of what education is and how to achieve it in a way that will encourage life-long learning. *Homeschooling for Excellence* by Micki and David Colfax gives you a good look at a successful homeschooling family, and much valuable advice. Raymond Moore's books remind one that in some cases late is better than early, and Marva Collins' book, *Marva Collins' Way,* tells of her experiences teaching children; it also gives great lists of materials that she thinks work well. Mary Kay Clark now has a specifically Catholic book on homeschooling in general. All of these books are useful, not only for general information, but also because they give some knowledge of methods, and list materials that have been found to work with children.

The second step is to acquire lists of other people's curricula. I recommend the curriculum lists of Seton Home Study, Our Lady of the

Rosary, Trinity Schools, Calvert Correspondence Course, and your own state's general requirements. Mary Pride's *Big Book of Home Learning* has information about other programs that might have curriculum lists that would interest you. (She also has the most complete listing of materials available for homeschoolers.) Designing your own curriculum involves seeing what other people have used successfully.

Once you have acquired all this information you will need to reduce it from a potential to an actual curriculum. This is where you use the background reading you have done. Think about the cause of causes, the end. Ask yourself, "What do I want for my children? What do I want them to achieve academically? Where are their interests? And what are their capabilities?"

This is the heart of designing your own curriculum, classical or otherwise. You need to be explicit about the ends you want to achieve. I'd like to tell you about my own goals so that you can see an example of how defining those goals will direct your choice of curriculum, giving you a plan to be implemented over the course of a number of years. Perhaps some of my reflections will also help you in more particular ways, by suggesting materials or methods that will be useful to you in designing the curriculum that fits your particular homeschooling situation.

While I was designing my curriculum I knew that I wanted ultimately what we all want, the eternal salvation of my children. Academically I wanted a truly Catholic intellectual formation. I hoped to instill a life-long love of learning, and to give my children the tools to pursue that learning.

More proximately, I wanted my children to be able to go to an academically excellent Catholic college and do well there. The ultimate end would be more likely to be achieved this way. Further, I was concerned that they receive a classical education at college, one that would incorporate the seven liberal arts and the disciplines they are ordered to, philosophy and theology. This kind of education is discussed in the essay by Dorothy Sayers that I mentioned earlier, "The Lost Tools of Learning."

There was a time when the excellence of liberal arts education was generally recognized; it was the education every informed person in western civilization received. Even now in homeschooling circles such an education is usually aimed for, sometimes under the title of liberal arts and sometimes not. Whatever it is called, what is desired is that each child be formed well in all the most important intellectual areas. Most of us want our children to study mathematics and English, science and religion, whatever our own special interests might be. I will talk in more detail about what is involved in such an education because I think most of us use something like this in determining our educational goals.

Most proximately, I wanted to teach the appropriate disciplines at the right ages for each child to reap the maximum benefit.

In the light of the ultimate end I knew that first importance must be given to spiritual formation. This would mean that the Church would have to be at the center of our lives as a family. We would go to daily Mass whenever possible, say the family Rosary, and talk about the Faith and its practical applications on a daily basis. While this is not an academic goal, it has an academic corollary. Our curriculum would always, at all levels, teach the doctrine of the Faith clearly. After all you can't apply what you don't know.

Further, I wanted to instill an attitude about learning that would lead to real interest in all parts and aspects of God's creation. I wanted my children to think that a new book or a new subject or a new project would be likely to be interesting. And I wanted them to get the best out of their scholastic endeavors, even when the material or the teaching might have some flaws. I thought, and I still think, that the best way to achieve this is to have that attitude yourself. Talk to your children about their academic work. Conversation with you is the most formative part of their intellectual life.

I think our family has succeeded in this. I do not mean that my children always think that this or that particular project is the most fun they could possibly be having. What they do think is that it is worthwhile, something they are glad to have done when it is finished, because they learned from it.

A case in point comes to mind. This past year I had my 9th graders read *The Red Badge of Courage* by Stephen Crane. It's an introspective book, and not all that easy to read. There was a certain amount of complaining about the book as we read and discussed it. However, when we finished the book I asked my two children what they thought about using it for their siblings. "Was it worth reading?" Both children said yes. My son said he learned something about how to deal with fear that he was glad to know and my daughter said she found the war discussions interesting! (It's not the kind of thing she ordinarily reads.) I was happy that even though it was not simply enjoyable for them they were able to get something valuable from reading and discussing it.

I also knew I wanted a curriculum which would demand a certain amount of rigor, something challenging enough to be stimulating. At the same time I knew that I would have to be careful to ensure some success for each child. Children, like all the rest of us, don't like to do what they are not good at.

And finally, I knew that the moral virtues would have to become habits, both in me and in the children, because one has to be disciplined and docile, obedient and willing, to learn well. I found that out in college, when I spent most of my first year learning how to study and learning to get my work done on time. For this reason I do have some deadlines for the children's work, usually for bigger projects like papers. Unlike some teachers, however, I will accept a reasonable excuse, like "But, Mom, while you were writing your talk, I did laundry and made dinner."

Which brings me to the next consideration. It seems to me likely that good Catholic colleges resemble one another in essentials; if a student is well-prepared for one he ought to be well prepared for the others. The curriculum at such a college should include those studies which are called (or used to be called) "general requirements" or liberal arts.

Traditionally, liberal arts education meant the education of a free man. A free man was understood to be one who could direct his own life (and the common life of the community), live a life of intrinsic and specifically human value (as opposed to the life of an animal or an instrument). The seven liberal arts were the introduction to such an education. These arts comprised the "trivium": grammar, rhetoric, and logic, and the "quadrivium": arithmetic, geometry, music, astronomy. These arts are ordered to the disciplines of philosophy and theology. Such an education is devoted to what is intrinsically worth knowing, for a man and for a Christian, whatever his way of life may be. Thus, to prepare for such an academic program is to prepare for any further learning which one may intend, and to prepare for a reasonable and Christian life for those who do not continue on to college.

Any particular interests that a child has can be taken into account as well. That can be done either by emphasizing the area of interest, if it is one of the subjects that ordinarily falls into such a general educational plan, or by adding a somewhat more specialized field. Two of my daughters like history very well and so I allow them to read more in that area, and do papers that deal with some aspect of history. In other words, for them I emphasize something that we would be doing anyway. My oldest son, on the other hand, enjoys computers. That was not originally part of my curriculum plan. Because of his interest, however, we do include some time with the computer in his daily work.

In general our curriculum has been designed with a liberal arts education in mind. Miss Sayers, in "The Lost Tools of Learning," directs our attention particularly to the arts of the Trivium: grammar, logic and rhetoric. She points out that two, at any rate, of these subjects are not subjects at all. They are methods of dealing with subjects. Grammar is a subject, in the sense that it means learning about a language, but language is a medium in which thought is expressed. In fact, the whole of the Trivium is intended to teach the tools of learning: methods of thinking, arguing, and expressing one's conclusions that will be applied to subjects. Now there must be subjects for these methods to be practiced upon. One cannot learn grammar without learning a language, or learn to argue and orate without arguing and orating about something. But the subjects are of secondary importance until the tools of learning have been refined.

The grammatical stage of learning is the first that follows the acquisition of the basic skills of reading, writing, and arithmetic. Once your child can do those his attention should be turned to the "grammar" of each subject he studies. This entails using his faculties for observation and memory in each subject. In language grammar it means learning an inflected language like Latin and practicing the chants. "Amo, amas, amat" is much like "eeny, meeny, miney, mo." This is what children do naturally at this stage; channel it into something constructive. In the other subjects, memorize. Train the imagination to retain information: fill the memory with a store of rich and varied images.

The next stage of the Trivium, the dialectical or logical, involves the discursive reason. The time to move into this level is when the student is able to appreciate and construct an intellectual argument. It seems to occur at about seventh grade for most children. At this point discussion and analysis become the heart of the curriculum.

The last stage of the Trivium is the rhetorical. This occurs somewhere around ninth grade and overlaps with the dialectical on one end, and the movement to subjects as subjects on the other. It seems to be characterized in the student both by the discovery that he needs to know more, and a resulting interest in and capacity for acquiring information. There is a new enjoyment of the poetical in literature, music and art. This combination of information and poetry gives the child an ability to express himself in elegant and persuasive language. In other words, he will need to have writing at the center of his curriculum.

In all three of these stages of the Trivium the student must have matter to work upon. The subjects should be chosen with a view to the disciplines of the liberal arts curriculum. In some cases this means doing what disposes the student to these studies; in other cases, it means making a beginning in them. These are the kinds of considerations you make in setting up your curriculum. You say, "I want my children to eventually have this kind of formation. What needs to be done to achieve it? Do I start teaching the subject itself now or do I do something that will enable them to do that subject well, later on?"

In terms of disposing children to these disciplines, there are two ways to go. One is to remove the obstacles to learning. Concentration on areas that might be trouble spots, such as grammar, music and mathematics, would be a good idea. Many who are otherwise good students have trouble with these subjects in college.

Even if one is not planning on a program of schooling that includes Latin in college, there is still a case to be made for studying Latin. Latin is an inflected language, where the endings of the words clearly indicate their function in a sentence. This means that the nature of the parts of speech is seen more clearly in Latin than in English. For this reason it is a good language to use in teaching grammar. It makes English grammar easier to understand.

With mathematics, the children should be skilled enough in all the ordinary operations so that they are able to simply concentrate on what is specifically new and challenging in their college classes. In a traditional liberal arts program, Euclidean geometry is studied. It is a theoretical discipline, well suited to the awakening intellectual power of a new college student. It's better to be able to make these universal considerations unhindered by purely technical difficulties.

Similarly, mathematical astronomy will proceed more smoothly if the operations of mathematics are second nature. For these reasons, our curriculum places emphasis on consistent application of mathematical skills and I insist every problem be reworked until it is right.

Preparation for the study of music is twofold. Mathematical ratios form much of the basis for discussion in the discipline. Clearly, mathematics is a preparation for this class. But so is the practical knowledge of how to read notes, and knowing what key a piece of music is in. Therefore, our curriculum includes some music. We use workbooks like *Music Reading, Ready to Use Activities Kit,* by Loretta Mitchell (15) and play recorder and piano. Also, because music is a wonderful thing in itself and something children will appreciate if exposed to, we always include music appreciation in the curriculum. There is a nice program available through St. Michael's in Carmichael, CA. It is called *The Music Masters* Series (6).

Since there are a number of papers required regularly in every college, writing skills are important. It is better to learn these early in one's educational career, and then be able to concentrate on the subject matter of one's paper, not having difficulties because of inadequate powers of expression. To acquire facility in writing, the important thing, it seems to me, is that the children write regularly and at some length. In the light of this consideration I have chosen an area each year in school that involves extensive writing. It is usually religion or history. In the high school years, writing becomes the heart of the curriculum, but for that to happen there should be writing practice from the beginning. I have found that book reports make my children unhappy and tend to deaden their interest in the book they have read, whereas a retelling of it, as for example, a description of the encounter of David and Goliath from the Philistine's point of view, or the story of St. Louis' crusade, is exciting.

Communication skills are very important in college. One needs to be able to speak clearly as well as write clearly. This means that it is helpful to have lots of experience of discussion. This is an area where busy homeschooling moms with pleasant, competent children need to decide firmly to do what is time consuming, but very important. Even if your children are able to go off, read their assignments and do their lessons without your help, it is important that they converse with you, important that you guide their understanding of the part of reality they encounter in their reading.

I use both Scripture readings and literature readings for discussion, and I encourage the children to state and defend their answers to the questions I ask. This is easier for them if their reading has been reflective. If they ask themselves some questions as they move through the book, anticipating a discussion where they will need to be able to present the heart of the position, they will be much better readers. I have found that having young children re-tell the story, and having older children prepare to discuss it helps to produce reflective reading. It also helps them to do better with factual questions.

The other way of preparing for the education at college involves the two disciplines that the seven liberal arts are ordered to. Our curriculum includes certain kinds of background information which will make the theology courses more immediately knowable, allowing the children to get involved right away in the heart of the matter. I have found that the *Baltimore Catechism* (4) is excellent preparation for theology because it is Saint Thomas distilled. Pick a topic, see what the *Baltimore Catechism* says and then compare it with the relevant article in the *Summa Theologiae*. St. Thomas is much more complete, but the basic position is in the catechism. Therefore, it seems to me that using the *Baltimore Catechism* in the early years makes St. Thomas much easier. One is already familiar with the terms and the general outline of the argument. And the format in the catechism is perfect for little children, who can memorize so much more easily than we can. Once learned, it stays with them for life.

Bishop John Myers said in a recent article, "Memorization of this sort allows a child to have a permanent space in mind and heart set aside for and dedicated to the things of God and of the Church. These essential elements are permanent acquisitions for the child, to refer to wherever he goes. He or she can retrieve them and ponder them from different aspects and in different life settings." Another preparation for theology is a familiarity with Sacred Scripture. St. Thomas and the other Fathers and Doctors of the Church most often use one part of Scripture to clarify and explain what is in another. All their theological works are full of Scriptural references. So I have included Sacred Scripture in my curriculum at nearly every level.

And lastly, the more advanced discussions of Catholic doctrine and practice found in books like *Of Sacraments and Sacrifice* by Fr. Clifford Howell and the Fr. John Laux high school series (14), provide a familiarity with the context within which theology must be understood.

Another discipline that I think you can prepare for in some measure is philosophy. Two different approaches help. Some acquaintance with philosophic terms is useful. The Seton Junior and Senior High School Religion courses do this. The other, and more important, approach is to provide your child with life experience.

To do philosophy well you need to have the beginning of wisdom, which enables you to make good judgments. Experience is essential, and can be gained directly, in the obvious manner of doing many (appropriate) things. This would include natural history. Science has always seemed to me something to be learned in detail later on; in the early years we emphasize natural history. This is a good area for field trips; both the zoo and natural history museums are a pleasant change from school books.

Philosophy can also be prepared for indirectly, by reading good books, both historical and fictional. In our curriculum I have included many books and allowed large chunks of time for reading. There are a number of resources for book lists of varying degrees of excellence. One is *Honey for a Child's Heart* by Gladys Hunt (3) and another is *Catholic Authors* (10), both the *4-sight* and *Crown editions*. More specifically historical texts can be found in *Books Children Love* by Elizabeth Wilson (3) and the short but first-rate journal, *In Review: Living Books Past and Present*, published by Bethlehem Books (9). The catalog of Greenleaf Press also has many interesting texts in this field.

Through an examination of the ultimate end I desired for my children's education, and the more particular end of going to college, a curriculum began to take shape. It would include Latin and English grammar, mathematics, literature, history, music, some philosophy, the *Baltimore Catechism*, and Sacred Scripture.

We would have discussions and I would endeavor to infuse those discussions with the sense of wonder and reverence for truth that could shape the attitudes of my children toward learning in general. I would require regular papers on subjects that would really be of interest.

Not all of these subjects would be covered every year, and not all would be covered in the same depth, but these would be the disciplines I would incorporate in my program. I would remember the method of the Trivium at each appropriate stage. With such a general plan we could make what we did do each year count in the overall intellectual formation of the children. You don't have to be so anxious about finishing each book (though it is certainly good to do so if possible), if you know that all of your efforts are coordinated and directed to a goal that is larger than accumulated knowledge in an individual subject.

You can see that my reflections on the ends I wanted to achieve guided my choice of subjects and methods. There were still further particular considerations to be made about what level was right for each subject and what method was appropriate. Those judgments can be made by examining the curriculum lists I mentioned earlier and by a certain amount of trial and error.

There was substantial general agreement among those lists with respect to what subjects were to be taught at what level. I would like to hit the highlights, not including too much detail.

Virtually all the lists included mathematics, reading, memorization, beginning writing skills and formative stories in the first three grades. This would be the very beginning of the future facility in mathematics, language arts, philosophy and theology that we wanted to achieve. I am inclined to the view that it is better to learn a little really well than a great deal superficially. For this reason I decided to concentrate on a thorough basic formation.

In kindergarten we try to become really familiar with the numbers. We use dominoes, dot-to-dot workbooks, the hundreds chart, and even a computer mathematics game or two. I use the A Beka math program (5) in the earliest grades. They have worked very well for us, and my children generally find themselves ready to do the *Saxon 65* (3) in fourth grade. I think this is because of the solid, sequential presentation of basic operations. Nevertheless there are other good mathematics programs, some emphasizing a more manipulative approach, such as Cuisenaire rods. Some children need to handle materials in order to learn; others can reason abstractly. Find out which kind of learner you are dealing with and use the appropriate kind of program. But whatever approach you choose, make sure the operations become second nature.

For beginning reading, in kindergarten, I use *Learning to Read in 100 Easy Lessons* by Engelmann, Haddox and Bruner (3) for about half of the book and then move on to *The Writing Road to Reading* by Romalda Spalding (3). The main point about what you select for reading is that it be phonetic in its approach. Using phonics will allow the child to read much more difficult material at an earlier age. It also helps with spelling and Latin. My husband, who has taught Latin for many years, says that all students in his experience who have had trouble reading and pronouncing Latin had been taught to read by the whole word method. He has made an informal study of the subject. When someone consistently stumbles over Latin pronunciation, and his spelling is "original," my husband discreetly asks what kind of reading instruction he has had. In such a case, the answer has never been phonics.

This early schooling is the stage Dorothy Sayers refers to as the "poll-parrot" stage, and it is a good time to begin the memorization of the questions and answers of the catechism. It is also a wonderful opportunity to introduce poetry. We pick a poem, work on it, say it for an obliging friend or relative, and then write it in a notebook reserved exclusively for that purpose. The child may illustrate it or not, depending on his inclination. We usually start with the poems of Robert Louis Stevenson, because they are so accessible to children. Then we move on to more difficult material. There is a book called *Favorite Poems Old and New* (3) that is a good anthology of poetry.

The poetry notebook is great fun as the children get older, because they have a book of their own making, filled with the poems they learned all through grade school, and they love it. It also helps them review without coercion, because they get to reminiscing. I leave those notebooks in an accessible place and every so often one of the children will pick a notebook up and leaf through it. They say, "Oh, I really liked this poem. Do you remember it?" And in that way they review the poems.

It is at this early stage that the child's broadest views of the world are being worked out. We all want our children to be clear about the difference between good and evil, truth and falsity. I think the things you pick to read to them and that you pick for their early reading are very important for this reason. Fairy tales, where there are clearly good guys and bad guys, are good for children. Books like *The Outlaws of Ravenhurst* by S. Mary Wallace instill a healthy respect for the Eucharist. Tales of King Arthur and his knights teach concepts of nobility and sacrifice. Stories of the saints are very important in these formative years because they present the supernatural end as the most compelling motivation.

History in these first grades seems to me best taught in somewhat the same mode as literature. That is, use materials that emphasize heroism, and individual accomplishment. Some of the books in the book lists I mentioned earlier are of this sort. Also, the third grade A Beka history book (5) is very good. It deals with outstanding individuals and the difference their contributions made to the founding of our country. A word of caution, however. After third grade, the A Beka history series becomes clearly protestant in tone and by sixth grade contains material that is specifically anti-Catholic.

We also read Bible stories in this early period. *The Children's Bible* (Golden Press) (1, 4) is an easy to understand version of this genre, and has kept the integrity of the stories. Whatever you use, emphasizing the goodness of certain individuals is important.

As I said earlier, science has always seemed to me something best learned in detail later on. The early years should be spent developing a love of nature. The zoo and natural history museums, as well as neighborhood walks, will encourage a real interest in natural history.

I mentioned earlier that for writing we prefer to pick a subject area and concentrate on writing in that area, rather than have writing as a separate subject. We often do Bible History this way, retelling the story after reading it. This exercise seems to strengthen the children's ability to see the story as a whole and to remember it. They like to illustrate their stories, too.

In the middle years, 4th–7th grade, the child becomes capable of mastering certain subjects and of coping with increasingly difficult material in others. All the lists I've looked at think that grammar should be taught with some rigor in this period. I myself find that sixth grade is the place to work intensely on grammar. Children seem to have matured enough at this point to enjoy parsing and diagramming, which are analytical skills.

Latin is also well suited to this stage. Here too, it seems that mastery of the fundamentals is most important. Vocabulary and forms can be taught and memorized in fourth and fifth grades, using Canon Press's *Latin Primer* and *Latin Grammar* (11). Another book, *Teaching English Grammar through Latin Background* by Ruth Wilson (22), works well in 7th grade. It consolidates English grammar from the year before, and teaches the first conjugation and first and second declensions very clearly. In the earlier years there are some texts that prepare the student for the study of Latin. *English from the Roots Up* by Joegil Lundquist gives a background in both Latin and Greek roots. This text can be used in second or third grade and will be the beginning of a lifetime of interest in words.

With respect to religion in these middle years I use a combination of things, all of which are ordered to those further goals I have already spoken about. Each year is divided into three parts: doctrine, Church history or Sacred Scripture, and lives of the saints. I continue to use the *Baltimore Catechism,* moving from the No. 1, which I have used in first through third grades, one section per grade, to the No. 2, which I use again one section per grade. In addition to the catechism I use some form of Bible History, either Fr. Ignatius Schuster's *Bible History* (14), or the *Bible Study Guide* by Dr. Donald and Mary Baker, or Sacred Scripture itself, with discussion questions of my own making. In fourth grade, the lives of the saints are also read and reported on, and in fifth grade I use the Faith and Life Catechism *I Believe* (4), which is excellent. In seventh grade I also use a Church History that all of my children have enjoyed, *The Story of the Church,* by Fr. George Johnson, Fr. Jerome Hannan and Sr. M. Dominica (14).

For writing in these middle years the important thing, it seems to me, is that the children write regularly and at some length. *Learning Language Arts Through Literature* (3) has some good ideas for creative writing. Retelling historical events has always been popular in my house. My oldest daughter wrote a history book in sixth grade that she greatly enjoyed, and she has kept it all these years. She read about different ancient civilizations and wrote down what she remembered in a notebook. She illustrated it with maps and made a cover for the front. That project made a major difference in her intellectual life. A friend's child decided to make a play about William the Conqueror. It was six pages, with many battle scenes. His whole family learned about that period of history from his writing effort. It matters more that there are some such writing exercises in your curriculum than that the children are always working on such a project. Pick a subject where you discern a lively interest and make that the focus of your writing curriculum.

Memorization at this stage can be more involved. Speeches from Shakespeare can be learned, and perhaps, with other homeschooling families, whole sections of Shakespeare's plays can be done. There is a book called *Shake Hands with Shakespeare,* by Albert Cullum, that edits the plays while retaining the flavor and much of the language, and makes it easy for a group of children to put on a Shakespeare play. If you are a purist you can keep the original language, but use this book as a guideline for cutting down the action. My children recently participated in a production of "A Midsummer Night's Dream," which was the joint effort of three homeschooling families. It was fun for them and they still enjoy quoting from the play.

There is a good science textbook series available called *Concepts and Challenges* (25). It has clear descriptions and an easy to follow format. A more hands-on approach is the *Tops* series (15). Each topic is covered by having the child do experiments involving only easily obtained materials. The unit on the balance is one of the more successful courses we've had. All of my older children are quite clear about the balance beam and how it works.

History is a subject that can be fascinating, or it can be deadly dull. Using a textbook with unit tests has a way of engaging the short term memory and nothing else. What works better is reading a chapter in a history text, and then reading other books, real books rather than textbooks, that cover that period of history. Then the information seems to come alive, and stay with you. Even in the later years, in high school, we have followed the same general procedure with history. *Books Children Love* by Elizabeth Wilson and the journal published by Bethlehem Books are both good sources for books of this kind. Also the catalog of Greenleaf Press has many important texts in this field. We acknowledge the cyclical nature of history teaching, and study American history in third, fifth and ninth grades. In fourth grade we study the exploration of the New World. Sixth and seventh grades are given to ancient civilizations, with an emphasis on Greece and Rome. In high school we study European history, concentrating on England and Spain, since these are the two that most directly affect our country.

*Ecce Romani* (16) is a series of books that incorporates the nature method of teaching Latin and analytic grammar, and it seems to work well at an eighth or ninth grade level. The text encourages learning the vocabulary from context as well as memorizing vocabulary lists. Both Seton and Our Lady of the Rosary offer a good Latin program which I have used for my high school curriculum.

In the later years, we concentrate more on reading well. Our religion, literature, art, and science classes all incorporate some discussion of more difficult points, retelling or making a synopsis of major issues, and some factual research — locating the place in the book where the author makes his point. It is in these subjects, about once a week for each, that I spend time with my older children. They do the preparation for the discussion on their own, and they do the other subjects they have on their own. I correct work and tests and discuss with them. I have always tried to work one-on-one with my children only in the areas where they need that kind of instruction.

I have a friend who homeschooled her oldest son through ninth grade. In tenth grade he went to a local high school. His mother watched him anxiously through the first week and then asked, "Josh, how is it?" He said, "It's so unbelievably easy. They tell you everything! I go to Algebra class and they say, 'Watch while I do this problem.' Then they put another one on the board and make sure you know how to do it. Then you do the rest of the problems in class and they'll answer any questions. School was never so simple before." I think Josh's experience is probably typical for homeschoolers. They are used to working on their own, at least as older students, and figuring things out. They are more independent learners, and do not need constant instruction. Our teaching role is more that of guidance and correction.

In this role, you should arouse interest in intellectual subjects by selecting good materials. Good literature and challenging texts are your best allies. I have found that a number of the Seton Home Study courses in tenth through twelfth grades are of real help. One is not required to be a full-time student with Seton; one can just select the courses that seem useful.

We have found Seton's English and religion programs for all three years to be outstanding. Their science courses are difficult but can be done. The Saxon mathematics can be done without their program, which simply consists of tests on the material. You can purchase the homeschool packet for the Saxon texts and the solution manuals and do just as well on your own. As I mentioned earlier, Seton has a Latin program that we like and it is nice to have someone else correcting the tests.

It also seems to me to be a good idea for children to deal with someone else as "teacher" before they go off to college. Using the Seton materials when they are helpful, and having an independent judge of the quality of a student's work, have been useful for our family.

It is a good idea to meet the homeschoolers in your area. It is helpful to have the support of other like-minded people. Often in talking over your successes and failures with others you will discover that your difficulty is a common one and, perhaps, that someone has discovered a solution. Or that your success is a solution to someone else's problem. In any case you will know you are not alone. *The Catholic Home Educator* is compiling a list of homeschoolers across the country. Their address is listed in the back of this book under suppliers (24).

I have some general advice about curriculum that is the result of my own mistakes over the years, which I hope you won't mind my adding. I love curricula, and I am always interested in new products; nevertheless, I've learned to stick with what works. If you have successfully taught your children to read using *Alphaphonics,* for example, don't abandon it because a friend is ecstatic about *Sing, Spell, Read and Write.* You already know how to use your program, and it works for you! On the other hand, throw out what doesn't work; sell it to a friend, it could be just what she needs. Or save it, maybe it will work for your next child. Each family, each child, and each teacher is unique. You can't tell for sure what is going to work for you except by trying it. When you find what does work, thank God for His blessings, and stick with it.

Evaluate your progress and success year by year, not moment by moment. Both you and your children will have ups and downs. Don't throw out good materials or despair of your ability because of a few bad days.

I have found that often when those bad days are too frequent over too long a period of time there are several corrective measures that might be considered. For one, easier materials can encourage success and a positive attitude. Challenge is important, but so is success. The right timing is also very important. Children mature at different rates and that does not in itself tell you much about innate ability. If you are trying a new concept or subject and it doesn't "take," wait and try again in a few months. I have a friend whose child taught himself to read at the age of three. My son of the same age learned to read when he was five and a half years of age. By the time they were six and a half there was no difference in their comprehension or reading ability. Another friend had a son who couldn't read well until he was nine. All three of these boys, who are now fourteen, are reading at the same level, and read the same material. A late reader may have a certain number of classics to catch up on, but that's no problem.

Aristotle says that virtue is a mean between moral extremes. For example, courage is neither rashness or timidity, but in between the two. I think school curricula should reflect this principle. There is a mean between no workbooks and all workbooks, between fun and drudgery, and between flexibility and firmness.

Lastly, you can probably tell that I like lists. Well, lists can make your school go more smoothly, not just in the yearly planning stage, but in your weekly and daily planning. Once your children can read, make them a list of their work for the week or the day and turn them loose. They can do what is on the list and come to you for help only in difficulties, or when they have finished the work that they are supposed to do by themselves and are ready to work with you. And after that, you can be otherwise occupied with ... laundry, dinner, and all the other things the valiant woman of faith must do.

## Where to get materials mentioned in the Introduction and not included specifically in the curriculum

*For the Children's Sake, Homeshooling for Excellence, Marva Collins' Way, The Big Book of Home Learning, Bible Study Guide* by Dr. Donald and Mary Baker, and *Sing, Spell, Read and Write* are available from *The Always Incomplete Catalog* (800) 377-0390.

"The Lost Tools of Learning" is found in *Recovering the Lost Tools of Learning* by Douglas Wilson, published by Canon Press (see supplier number 11).

*The Red Badge of Courage* by Stephen Crane is available through any bookstore.

*Shake Hands with Shakespeare* by Albert Cullum and *Of Sacraments and Sacrifice* by Fr. Clifford Howell, S.J., are unfortunately out of print. There are used copies out there, however, and these are books worth looking for. Loome's Theological Booksellers (612) 430-1092, has had Fr. Clifford's book in the past.

*Catholic Homeschooling* by Mary Kay Clark and *The Outlaws of Ravenhurst* by Sister Mary Wallace are available through Town Book Fairs (303) 493-6311.

The following are phone numbers for the lists I recommended: Seton Home Study (703) 636-9990, Our Lady of the Rosary (502) 348-1338, Trinity School (219) 287-5590, and Calvert Correspondence Course (301) 243-6030.

To acquire your own state's general requirements write to your state's Dept. of Education. You could call your local school district for the address, or the library.

# Curriculum Suggestions

———— ❊ ————

I T IS THE ABILITY TO THINK that is our goal in a classical curriculum; we want our children to acquire the art of learning. It is not the number of facts they are acquainted with that measures educational success, but what they are able to do with the facts, whether they are able to distinguish, to follow an argument, to make reasonable deductions from the facts, and finally to have a right judgment about the way things are.

Such a view of education has some practical consequences that are discussed at various stages in this curriculum. At this point it is appropriate to reflect on one of them. The question of what you should expect to do with a child, and what he can do on his own, is important.

The main goal of the early school years is to learn the basic skills of reading, writing, and simple arithmetic. These are the first tools for any further learning. The subjects you use to acquire and practice these tools are, in a sense, secondary. This is so much the case that the mother of a large number of homeschooling children, who is only able to do religion, reading, simple arithmetic and basic letter formation with her youngest grades should not worry that they are educationally neglected. The natural stimulation of a busy household will supply for the other subjects. Once a child can read he is able to be an independent learner.

You should encourage him to take charge of his education, where he can. This will foster the ability to learn that you are intending him to acquire. At the same time, classes require supervision and some discussion. Have your child do the reading, preparation and any exercises on his own, with an understanding that he will have some specific time with you to go over what he has prepared. Disciplines that are of particular difficulty for a given child, or classes where the method requires the parent's presence, should be done when you are going over his other, prepared work. This makes it possible to combine the virtues of different methods of teaching. There is one-on-one instruction with immediate feedback, but there is also self-direction.

This also makes it possible to teach a larger number of classes to more children. Start working with your youngest child first, and when he is finished with his school work move on to the next child. Do with each child only what he needs you to do with him. Work with two children together when possible. Multiple classes can be easily taken care of in this way, which is the way the one room school house used to work.

Clearly, the first requirement in such a plan is to learn the skills necessary for any further learning. Concentrate on reading well, learning to write, both in terms of letter formation and powers of expression. Spend time acquiring facility in addition and subtraction. If these things are learned well, all the rest of one's school time will be much more profitable. For these reasons I do not emphasize science or history in kindergarten, first or second grade.

Even in third through sixth grades, studies will be ordered to the acquisition of a certain kind of formation, where observation, memory, and the beginning of definition are the heart of the curriculum. This formation is more important than the various subjects studied. These will provide material for the formation. Thus, if you begin to be overwhelmed with the chores and duties of a big household, and you do not get done all that you would like to do, or had planned to do, educationally, don't worry about it. Make what you are able to do count by employing the methods appropriate to the stage of formation of your child.

Also, remember that your children learn from you by your conversation and example all day long, every day. Your Faith, which informs your life, will inform theirs if they are with you. Your delight in God's creation will communicate to them the wonders God has given us, and gratitude for them. It will inspire your children with an interest in learning.

Additionally, in a large family the children must help with the household chores, as a matter of survival. They learn to cook, do laundry and clean. This is great practical education, and contributes in its own way to theoretical education, because the children learn about the common good from direct experience. It can also be used by you as a time for discussion; doing laundry or dishes together provides opportunities for conversation that might otherwise be scarce. In such a family the children see the good of the whole as their good, they see themselves as working with you for a common enterprise, as a comrade, rather than as part of a peer group to which adults do not belong. This attitude, along with the fact that you get to learn new things (indeed, if you are like me, probably have to learn new things), are the two biggest benefits of homeschooling.

The classical curriculum is thus chiefly concerned with formation. The stages of formation are discussed within this curriculum at the beginning of each section. Though the stages are not rigidly tied to age or grade level, I have chosen to discuss Grammar before third, Dialectic before seventh and Rhetoric before tenth grade. Look at those discussions when you are choosing your curriculum and think about what stage is appropriate for your child. All of my curriculum suggestions are intended to be flexible. Ideas for fifth grade may work well for sixth or fourth, while art and music suggestions are often applicable in every grade. I offer these suggestions as things that have worked for us, at about the grade levels listed.

All of the following text suggestions are just that: suggestions. Since every family and every student is different there isn't any one text that is the only text that will work in any given subject. The texts I mention here have worked well for me and in most cases for a number of other homeschoolers in my area. Nevertheless what seems to me more important is the general advice, and the goals to be achieved. If you know of something better that will achieve these goals, use it and tell me about it!

You will notice in examining these lists that certain areas are not mentioned at all, for example, physical education and penmanship. Still others are presupposed to any formal learning.

Physical skills incorporating large motor development are very important for little children. Learning to skip, ride a tricycle, walk a balance beam, and swing on a swing are examples of abilities that should be encouraged. I don't address these skills in my curriculum because I think that you don't need my advice in this area. Give children time and space and a little example and they will develop these faculties on their own. Homeschooling, because it is such an efficient use of school time, leaves much more free time for such play.

As your children grow, participation in recreational programs will exercise physical skills. Soccer, Irish step dancing, baseball, track, swimming, and gymnastics are all programs my own children have been involved in through the years.

I won't mention penmanship in what follows because my own approach doesn't change much through the years. If I address it here I will have said what I have to say about it. In *The Writing Road to*

*Reading* by Romalda Spalding, there is a clear, easy manuscript taught. We use this and practice the letters as they are introduced and used in the text. When the time comes for cursive writing, which can vary radically from child to child, I have used the A Beka third grade cursive text. It's a pretty script, and the exercises are pleasant. Thereafter, at the beginning of each year, or if someone is getting sloppy, we review. I have just seen the Seton penmanship text and it is very appealing, with Catholic references and attitudes. I plan to order some for next year to have around the house for practice when it is necessary.

Finally, there are certain activities that are presupposed to the suggestions that follow. Putting together puzzles, following the directions for Lego assemblies, exploring textures and smells, playing simple games with color matches and doing finger plays all involve pre-reading skills, and should certainly be done with your children. I would like to point out that most children do these things, at least many of them, on their own, but the guidance of an adult or older sibling will direct a child to a specific skill more clearly.

All resources in this list are followed by a number which indicates which of the suppliers, listed on the last page, carries this item.

# Kindergarten Curriculum

**Sources for items followed by a number in parentheses may
be found at the back of the book under the suppliers list.**

RELIGION — *The Children's Bible* (GOLDEN PRESS) (1,4)

Read from *The Children's Bible* twice a week. Begin each class
with the child's retelling of the previous story. Write it down in an
artist's sketch book. On alternate days have the child illustrate his
stories. At the end of the year he will have his own Bible.

The goals of this class are to become familiar with the Bible and
internalize the stories and doctrine of the early books of the Old
Testament, as well as develop listening and "re-telling" skills.

MATHEMATICS — *Golden Step Ahead Workbooks* (2), NUMBER FLASH-
CARDS (2), *An Easy Start in Arithmetic* BY RUTH BEECHICK (3)

Twice a week work on familiarity with numbers. The idea here is to
have the numbers mean something real. Using beans or Legos helps
to make the concepts concrete. By the end of the year the child will
probably be able to count to 100, recognize the numerals to 25
easily, and further than that with some help. Simple addition and
subtraction problems will be easy to do.

READING — *How to Teach Your Child to Read in 100 Easy Lessons* BY
ENGELMANN, HADDOX AND BRUNET (3), *Honey for a Child's Heart*
BY GLADYS HUNT (3) FOR LITERATURE

Have short reading lessons four times a week. There are other good
phonetic texts available and the most important aspect of teaching
reading is that it be done phonetically. I like this text because it
teaches blending so well; you move beyond the /c/ ... /a/ ... /t/
stage to "cat" easily and quickly.

Don't expect to finish this text in a year. Some children may
move that quickly but most of those I have known take longer. The
purpose of this class is to learn to read on an "Easy Reader" level,

and that level is reached before the end of the book. At this time of life what you read to your children is much more important, because it is much more formative, than what they read to themselves. Ideally there should be long, cozy, evening reading sessions with the whole family. If your kindergartner doesn't learn to read this year, or in the next three years, it won't finally make much difference in his life. But the saint stories, the tales of noble actions performed by noble people, the fairy tales will make a lifelong difference.

## SCIENCE — NO TEXT

Visits to the zoo, natural history museum, beach, and walks around the neighborhood are all occasions for science discussion. Science at this point could be better described as natural history, or getting to know the world around you. Raising animals, sprouting beans, helping in a garden are simple, natural ways of becoming familiar with the physical world.

## POETRY — *A Child's Garden of Verses* BY ROBERT LOUIS STEVENSON (1)

Work for 5 minutes or so every day on a poem. When the poem is learned make an occasion for the child to recite it to the family, or get a few families together for this purpose. This gives the child an opportunity to practice stage presence (a disposing factor in acquiring rhetoric) at an early age, before concern about what other people might think sets in. If you can keep it up even your shy sixth grader will think that reciting poetry for the enjoyment of other people is part of life. It is also an incentive for getting the poem "down cold" and that will mean better retention. I have kept a record of each child's poems through the years, and the children who enjoy drawing have illustrated their poems. Illustrated or not, the record of poems learned is a treasure for the children to enjoy all their lives.

## ART — *Mommy, Its a Renoir* (EASY LEVEL) (3), DRAW BIBLE PICTURES

*Mommy, Its a Renoir* is an art appreciation course that has numerous levels. This level contains pairs of pictures by the same artist. The child is asked to match identical picture pairs or similar picture pairs. My own little children have enjoyed this course. When they have mastered the intended goals of the class we have gone on to do other things with the pictures. I have them make up a story about the picture, or describe the picture and then I try to pick out the right postcard from what they say. We look for other pictures by the same artist and talk about any similarities we can see. *For the Children's Sake* by Susan Schaeffer MacCauley (3) has a very good section on art appreciation that is well worth reading. The immediate goal is to help the children be attentive to and begin to enjoy great works of art. But you also begin to develop their vocabulary, powers of expression and imagination by conversing with them about the pictures.

Drawing illustrations for the Bible book the children are writing in Religion will help them remember the stories as well as give them an opportunity to express their thoughts and feelings in a visual medium.

## MUSIC — HYMN SINGING

Even little children can learn the hymns that are sung at Church, or the ones that ought to be. This can be a family project, which will encourage participation in a Church setting, as well as make uncertain singers feel that their deficiencies are masked.

## TENTATIVE SCHEDULE FOR KINDERGARTEN

Allow about 45 minutes each day for school. This is ample time for formal subjects for such young children.

| MON. | TUES. | WED. | THURS. |
|---|---|---|---|
| POETRY | POETRY | POETRY | POETRY |
| READING | READING | READING | READING |
| RELIGION | RELIGION | RELIGION | RELIGION |
| (DRAWING) | MATH | (DRAWING) | MATH |

EVENINGS — LITERATURE, MUSIC

# First Grade Curriculum

**Sources for items followed by a number in parentheses may be found at the back of the book under the suppliers list.**

RELIGION — *St. Joseph's First Communion Catechism* (4)

Read and discuss each chapter of the catechism. Have the child memorize the questions and answers, which will be easy for him to do because little children are like sponges. They soak in information and keep it. Also, memorization done now will pay off in a big way later because it develops a habit of retention. In addition to developing a retentive imagination, learning the answers in the catechism word for word is a good thing to do because the very words of the catechism are formative. Those words express "this" truth well and train the mind in a certain way of thinking. Use game formats to check and reinforce memorization (e.g. have the child supply the question for your answer, or give points and prizes for a certain number of correct answers).

Read saint's lives aloud (e.g. *A Children's Book of Saints* by Hugh Ross Williamson (1)). Have the child re-tell the story, or draw a series of illustrations for the stories, or make a book (with your help) of retold and illustrated stories.

MATHEMATICS — *Arithmetic 1* (A BEKA) (5)

This is a good book to use because it has a spiral approach to learning concepts. Once learned, a concept is practiced on a daily basis. The child never has a chance to forget how to do it.

READING — *Teach Your Child to Read in 100 Easy Lessons* BY ENGELMANN, HADDOX AND BRUNER (3), OR *Alphaphonics* BY SAM BLUMENFIELD (3), OR *The Writing Road to Reading* BY ROMALDA SPALDING (3)

The basic point about teaching reading is still to use phonics, which all of the above do. As I said, *100 Easy Lessons* is easy to use and satisfying because the child begins to read quickly. I can vouch for its effectiveness. However, I use Spalding after my children are able to read because the phonics principles are taught so clearly in it. There is a helpful supplementary book for use with Spalding called *Teaching Reading at Home* by Wanda Sanseri (3).

LITERATURE — READ ALOUD LITERATURE ON A REGULAR BASIS. *Honey for a Child's Heart* BY GLADYS HUNT (3) HAS A GOOD LIST OF BOOKS. *In Review*, A QUARTERLY BY BETHLEHEM BOOKS (9), HAS GREAT LISTS AND REVIEWS OF CHILDREN'S LITERATURE. *Catholic Authors, 4-Sight Edition* (10), HAS LISTS OF CATHOLIC LITERATURE, MANY OF THEM OUT OF PRINT, BUT WORTH KNOWING ABOUT FOR VISITS TO USED BOOK STORES AND THRIFT STORES. ALSO, SOME OF THEM ARE BACK IN PRINT OR WILL BE.

Concentrate on filling your child's imagination with stories of individuals who choose good in the face of difficulties. Beautiful language, while more difficult to listen to, both develops their vocabulary and their ear for language.

SCIENCE — NO TEXT

Continue with the method of the previous year. Talk about the world around you and visit interesting natural history places. Perhaps you could make a bird feeder or acquire a cockatiel. An aquarium is fairly easy to maintain and provides a focus for natural history. Whatever you do, always be interested yourself. If you notice a spider web, point it out, and use the occasion for a little research on spiders. This class is not formal, or scheduled, but it is important in this way: it is an opportunity for you to encourage a lifelong love for all of God's amazing creation. The natural history information and observational skills acquired now will help all through the school years, even when the subjects of philosophy and theology become the center of interest.

POETRY — *A Child's Garden of Verses* BY ROBERT LOUIS STEVENSON (1), OR *Favorite Poems Old and New* (3).

Every day spend 5-10 minutes memorizing a poem. When it is memorized write it down in a separate notebook. Keep the notebook and at the end of the year you will have a personalized record of all the poems learned.

Poems we have found to work well are "Windy Nights," "Bed in Summer," "Foreign lands," "Where Go the Boats," "The Land of Counterpane," "My Shadow," "The Wind," "The Moon," "The Swing," "The Hayloft," "The Lamplighter," and "The Cow," all by Robert Louis Stevenson. Poetry provides another opportunity to exercise the imagination and to train it. Recalling lines of poetry requires some discipline, even though poetry is easier to recall than prose. Memorizing poems develops, painlessly, a facile and obedient memory.

## ART — *Mommy, It's a Renoir* (INTERMEDIATE LEVEL) (3)

This is a Montessori art appreciation program. It develops observational skills and appreciation for beautiful things, and introduces children to great paintings. We usually use the postcards according to the text until the child has mastered the skills specifically intended by the program. Then we invent other uses for the pictures that will further those goals. Talking about the picture, distinguishing the forms from the colors, discussing the feelings evoked, the smells and sounds suggested, will give a certain distinction to your child's observations. It will also begin to develop an analytical power, thinking about why certain colors or figures are used, how they function in the picture as a whole. You don't need to discuss that explicitly, but by doing it, this year and in subsequent years, you will as a matter of fact develop that power.

*Aesops Fables* can be used for art. Read a fable to the child and have him retell it to you. Then write down what he says and have him illustrate it. Later, when he is comfortable writing, you can write down sentences for him to copy, either of his composition or yours. This stage gives him valuable practice in hand-eye coordination. Finally, he can write his own summary. Keep these papers together and your child will have his own illustrated version of *Aesop* at the end of the year.

This particular activity incorporates many skills that are important to this stage of development. It encourages re-telling, which requires a concept of the whole, develops powers of expression, involves small motor coordination as well as hand-eye coordination, and incorporates literature, art, and composition. Additionally, because the fables are short, it doesn't take much time, and so far everyone has enjoyed it!

Music — *The Music Masters* Series, Part # 1 (6), *Wee Sing* Tapes (3)

Use *The Music Masters* Series for music appreciation. It consists of a series of tapes or CDs that introduce the child to Classical music, with information about the composer's lives. Conversing with the child after the tape is over allows you to talk both about the way the composer dealt with difficulties and about his gifts. It will also help fix that composer in the child's mind so that you can refer to him as you listen to his music. "This is by Mozart, do you remember him?" Clearly, it is more important to listen to the music than to know about the composer, and the aim of music appreciation is to become familiar with, and to enjoy, beautiful and important pieces of music. But learning about the composer can help achieve that end and this is a good time to begin.

## Tentative Schedule for First Grade

Allow about 1 ½ hours each day for school. This is ample time for formal subjects for young children.

| Mon. | Tues. | Wed. | Thurs. |
|---|---|---|---|
| Math | Math | Math | Math |
| Phonics | Phonics | Phonics | Phonics |
| Religion | Religion | Religion | Religion |
| Poetry | Art | Poetry | Poetry |

Evenings — Literature, Music

# Second Grade Curriculum

**Sources for items followed by a number in parentheses may be found at the back of the book under the suppliers list.**

RELIGION — *St. Joseph's Baltimore Catechism No. 1* (4), LIVES OF THE SAINTS (4)

Read and discuss the first fourteen chapters of the catechism. Memorize the questions and answers. I recommend doing a chapter in the catechism and working on the questions over a two week period. The second week, when you are working on memorization only, can also involve a study of the lives of the saints.

The same reasons given earlier for memorizing still apply; it develops a habit of retention, it encourages attention to detail, and the very words of the catechism are formative. Those time honored answers are formulas in terms of which one's very thought is formed.

The catechism has exercises at the end of every chapter, along with Scripture readings, which will aid the comprehension of the lessons in the chapter. Spend some time each day on the questions and answers, but the other activities can be spread out over the week. On Monday discuss the chapter. On Tuesday do the True/False and Fill in the Blanks exercises. On Wednesday and Thursday review the discussion questions.

The next week review the material once, in addition to memorizing the questions and answers, but then spend some time with saint stories.

Your child's First Communion will probably take place sometime during this year. The *First Communion Catechism* from last year has been a good preparation for this great event. Review that catechism, especially the parts dealing with Confession and Communion, as your child's First Confession and Communion draw near. Read the book *Patron Saint of First Communicants, The Story of Blessed Imelda Lambertini* by Mary Fabyan Windeatt (14) with your child. Teach some special prayers for after Communion, per-haps *Soul of Christ, Sanctify Me* (a favorite prayer of St. Thomas Aquinas). The Ten Commandments will be studied in detail next year, but the examination of conscience in the *First Communion Catechism* involves a practical application of the Commandments in a way appropriate for little children.

MATHEMATICS — *Arithmetic 2* (A BEKA) (5), *Math-It* BY E.W. BROOKS (23)

This text will help the child learn to read, write, count, and use numbers up to 1000. It will present the concept of place value to the hundred's place. It reviews counting in groups (twos, fives, tens) up to 30 and introduces counting by groups up to 100. Simple addition and subtraction are reviewed and the child learns to carry and borrow. The multiplication tables are introduced by presentation of the fives and tens. Word problems are dealt with regularly, so that the child is able to "translate" from words to numerical operations. Telling time is reviewed from last year, and there is ample opportu-nity to practice reading a clock. There is some work done with money, both counting and writing amounts. And all of this is done in such a way that once learned the child never has a chance to forget it, because there will be some problems of each kind in every lesson.

*Math-It* provides practice in addition facts much like drill sheets would, but it doesn't involve writing. This is good for two reasons. Some children, especially boys, find writing difficult at this stage. With *Math-It* they don't have to write. Also mental math is a specific skill that should be exercised.

Math needs to be done everyday to acquire facility with num-bers.

READING AND WRITING — *Writing Road to Reading* BY ROMALDA SPALDING (3), STEP UP BOOKS (RANDOM HOUSE) (1), I CAN READ BOOKS (HARPER TROPHY) (8), *Learning Language Arts Through Literature* (RED BOOK) (3)

*The Writing Road* is not the easiest text to use and if your child is reading fluently you may not think it is necessary. I don't know that it is, but I surely have enjoyed it. The phonics rules and decoding skills taught in the text are by far the clearest and most complete I have ever dealt with. There is a companion book by Wanda Sanseri called *Teaching Reading at Home* that makes the text more accessible and gives a sequential table that helps you know what to do when.

One of my children had begun to read by the time she was seven, but was not confident, and because of that, did not enjoy reading. I used *Writing Road* and taught her the phonograms, the 72 smallest units of sound in English, and her reading took off. It gave her the assurance that reading involved comprehensible rules, which when learned would unlock the meaning of the words. Prior to learning the phonograms she felt it was just chance what sound a particular combination of letters might make.

Not all of my children have felt the same way, but I think they have all benefited from *The Writing Road.* As a spelling text for the child who has difficulties with spelling I think it is unequaled. It contains a list of the 1,000 most used words in the English language, divided into skill levels. The words are broken apart and marked in the way that a good natural speller would do. Thus you provide for the poorer speller the tools that the good speller uses without reflection. Even for the good speller a list of the most common words in our language is helpful.

Once the child is able to read he should be supplied with appropriate reading materials. *The Writing Road to Reading* has a fine reading list for the beginning reader and beyond, and the Step Up Books and I Can Read Books are also sources of material. Carolyn Haywood's *Penny and Eddie* series of books and Gertrude Chandler Warner's *Boxcar Children* (1) books have also been big hits in my house at this stage.

*Learning Language Arts Through Literature* is a suitable text for beginning writing skills. You should feel free to use it as much or as little as you like. There is a five day a week plan built into the text, and it is a good plan. I use the text more loosely. However you choose to use it, the best thing about this series is the emphasis on learning about writing by close attention to well written passages.

LITERATURE — *Honey For a Child's Heart* BY GLADYS HUNT (3)

Reading to your child is still extremely important at this level of language development. You will be doing factual reading and discussing in History. In the evenings you might consider reading stories featuring families. *Mary Poppins* by P.L. Travers, *The Narnian Chronicles* by C.S. Lewis, *The Railway Children* by E. Nesbit, and *All of a Kind Family* by Sydney Taylor are some examples of this type of book. They are not factual, but they are stories about recognizable characters in a family setting. They offer a contrasting way to learn truths about people.

SCIENCE — *Explorations with Earth Science* (FEARON TEACHER AIDS) (5), USBORNE *Science with Plants* (2)

These texts are investigative in character, and can be used in a way consonant with the science of the previous two years. The emphasis is on learning about the world around you by observation and conversation. There are simple experiments suggested in the texts that lend themselves to this approach. We usually spend time one day a week, or possibly every other week, on this class. But in the spring our family makes regular visits to the zoo, beach, botanical gardens, and natural history museum.

HISTORY/GEOGRAPHY — FAMILY HISTORY (YOU), D'AULAIRE'S BIOGRAPHIES (8), *Childhood of Famous Americans* SERIES (8), USBORNE BOOKS (2), STATES AND CAPITALS FLASHCARDS (2), *Learning About U.S. Geography* BY BARBARA GRUBER (FRANK SCHAFFER PUBLICATIONS) (2)

It seems to me that the right way to start the subject of history is to use an example that will be comprehensible to little children. Family history, especially the child's own early history, is understandable and intensely interesting to him. One can move from that to some analogous understanding of the history of our country's early leaders.

The D'Aulaire biographies are entertaining and informative. While you read the text to your child he will be able work on listening skills, especially if you have him re-tell parts of the story. This encourages comprehension, oral expression, sequencing, and interest. The D'Aulaire biographies include *Pocahontas, Benjamin Franklin, George Washington,* and *Abraham Lincoln.*

*The Childhood of Early Americans* series is written on a second or third grade level. I think that these should be used when the child is reading fairly well on his own. If that is not yet, wait until next year. These are nice books for reading practice because they exercise the skill of reading on a subject that you want to cover anyway.

Many children enjoy the way the Usborne books are laid out. You might look some over to see if they fit your needs.

*Learning About U.S. Geography* is an intelligently laid out workbook. It introduces basic geographical concepts (like mountains, lakes, deserts, continents) in a simple, single page per concept format. If you don't use it this year I would recommend using it next year. It moves the child easily into the next stage of learning, the grammatical stage, with respect to this subject. I'll be talking about that soon.

Learning the states and capitals is also part of this next stage of learning. Second and third graders can begin to acquire, by memory, various lists. The states and capitals constitute a list that is useful to know, and do eventually lead to a better geographical knowledge of our country than many people have. I like flashcards for this exercise but a simple list will do, or *Geo-Safari* (15), or a state board game. *Learning About U.S. Geography* has a list of states and capitals.

I work a couple days each week on the memorization, but the rest of the material is adequately covered in the course of the year by having class once a week.

Poetry — I recommend continuing the previous years' program.

Some poems that have worked well for us are "The Land of Storybooks" by Robert Louis Stevenson, "The Owl and the Pussycat" by Edward Lear, "The Christening" by A.A. Milne, "The Duel" by Eugene Field, "The Song of Mr. Toad" by Kenneth Grahame, "Stopping by the Woods on a Snowy Evening" by Robert Frost, Psalm 100, Psalm 23, and the prayer "Soul of Christ, Sanctify Me."

Art — *Mommy, It's a Renoir* (Advanced level) (3), visits to art museums, crocheting

Though the material is slightly more difficult in this level of *Mommy, It's a Renoir,* the use of the material is basically the same as in previous years. One addition to my earlier suggestions is to add rough placement sketches by the child as a way of encouraging close observation. Have him look at the picture carefully and then turn it over. On a piece of blank paper have him sketch the picture, with little concern for form but with attention to the placement of the forms in the picture. When he turns it over and looks at the picture again he will notice things about the picture that he just never saw before.

Another way of expanding the exposure to beautiful works of art is by visiting a nearby museum. Such a visit is much more profitable with a little preparation. Obtain prints of some of the pictures that are in the museum. Use those prints for your art exercises, and spend enough time with them so that the child is really familiar with the paintings. Then go see the paintings in the museum. The encounter with the original will be delightful because it will involve recognition. It will be like meeting an old friend.

Simple crocheting is a skill that little children can master. They love to make long chains and will decorate the Christmas tree for you if you let them. Crocheting exercises the fine motor muscles and encourages coordination.

Art activities can be done once a week and the activities should be varied week by week.

MUSIC — *Easy Recorder Tunes* (USBORNE) (3), *Let's Learn Music* # 1 (HAYES) (22), *The Music Masters* SERIES, PART # 2 (6)

If you learn to play the recorder the music text will make more sense. Piano would do just as well, or any other instrument. If the child spends much time with an instrument you could dispense with the text because it would be superfluous. However, if you don't plan on music lessons right now, this text, with the recorder, will give your child the basic idea of the structure of the music he is listening to in the *Music Masters* Series. He will begin to understand musical time, notation, and recorder technique. He will also learn to play some simple tunes on the recorder.

I think that learning to play an instrument is a help to listening to music, and it is fun in itself. But I think that listening to good music and enjoying it is more important. Concentrate on that.

## Tentative Schedule for Second Grade

From this point on the amount of time spent each day on school subjects will vary so much from child to child that I no longer make suggestions for time allotments. Try for a mean between too much and too little time for your child. That is very general advice, but it is true.

| Mon. | Tues. | Wed. | Thurs. | Fri. |
|------|-------|------|--------|------|
| Math | Math | Math | Math | Math |
| English | English | English | English | English |
| Religion | Religion | Religion | Religion | Religion |
| Music | Art | Science | History | |

Evenings — Literature

# NOTES

# The Grammatical Stage

# The Grammatical Stage

THUS FAR IN THIS PROPOSED CURRICULUM there has been a certain similarity of approach in most subjects. Variation in the classes has been supplied by the matter rather than by a difference in method, because the subjects have been seen as occasions to practice the skills appropriate to this level of formation. You practice reading and writing by doing it, which means reading and writing about something. But the primary aim is to learn to read and write, not to accumulate information. Of course religious doctrine is of the utmost importance in itself, and is not just an occasion to practice skills. Nevertheless, it doesn't hurt to have the child practice oral reading while going over the catechism chapters with you.

In the next stage of educational formation, extending from 3rd or 4th grade through 7th, the subjects again provide practice for the method.

Miss Sayers, in "The Lost Tools of Learning," calls this stage the "Poll-Parrot," "in which learning by heart is easy and, on the whole, pleasurable.... At this age, one readily memorizes the shapes and appearances of things; one likes to recite the number-plates of cars; one rejoices in the chanting of rhymes and the rumble and thunder of unintelligible polysyllables; one enjoys the mere accumulation of things."

This natural stage of development corresponds to the Grammar of the Trivium, which I discussed in the introduction. In a classical education the Trivium was seen as the method of education. It was presupposed to the Quadrivium, which provided subjects. A classical education was designed to produce people who knew how to learn, who had acquired the "tools of learning."

Grammar pertains first and most specifically to language, and to some particular language. The faculties of observation and memorization, which are so lively at this time, make learning a language relatively easy and enjoyable. I prefer Latin for a variety of reasons. It is inflected, which means the nature of the speech is much more clearly seen in it. It is the key to the structure and vocabulary of the Romance languages, it underlies the technical vocabulary of the sciences and much of the literature of our culture. Further, learning to chant the paradigms is such fun at this age. "Amo, amas, amat" is very reminiscent of "eeny, meeny, miney, mo." Lastly, there are good texts available for third or fourth grade on up.

It is easy to see what Grammar means with respect to language. It seems to me that there is an analogous meaning in relation to the other subjects. In each case, what is emphasized is the method of observation and memorization exercised on different disciplines. This approach both trains the mind and gathers together material for use in the next part of the Trivium, the Dialectic. What is attempted is not a mere accumulation of facts, but a method of learning. Nonetheless, specific details will be learned.

At this stage, such a curriculum will look similar to any other; the difference will be primarily in the acknowledgment that the method — the training of the mind by observation and the imagination by memorization — is more fundamental than the subjects on which it is exercised.

# Third Grade Curriculum

**Sources for items followed by a number in parentheses may be found at the back of the book under the suppliers list.**

RELIGION — *Child's Bible History* BY F.J. KNECHT, D.D. (14), *Baltimore Catechism No. I* (4), TEN COMMANDMENTS BOOK (BY YOUR CHILD)

At this grammatical stage it is appropriate to learn about salvation history in outline. The narrative of Creation, the Fall, and our Redemption is presented simply and enjoyably in the Bible history stories. Complete understanding of the material is not what is aimed for; rather the basic story should be known and remembered.

One suggestion for achieving this, which incorporates practice in other necessary skills, is the making of a Bible storybook. Reading the story either aloud or to himself, and then writing a summary of the material, familiarizes the child with the history and encourages him to follow a logical sequence in telling or writing stories. It provides an area for writing where the child has something to say. It can become an illustrated text which you bind, incorporating both drawing and crafts.

Last year the first section of the catechism was studied. This year the second section is considered. Since the commandments are studied in some detail, another activity that is helpful is a Ten Commandments Book. Highlight the positive side of the commandment, i.e. Thou shall not kill enjoins upon men a concern for and caretaking of the people around us. Have the child write the commandment at the top of a page and then draw a picture of what it means he should do. This is an exercise that employs fine motor skills and can be used to draw attention to color harmonies, simply by talking about which colors go well together. It also helps the child remember the commandments.

Alternate these activities. One week work on the catechism chapter, discussing it one day and doing the chapter exercises the next day. On the two following days, in addition to going over the questions and answers for memorization, you could work on the commandment book. The next two weeks could be given to Bible history, while the questions and answers of the catechism are being memorized. This way there are three weeks for memorization of the chapter questions, and there is variety in the child's class.

MATHEMATICS — *Arithmetic 3* (A BEKA) (5), *Calculadder* BY EDWIN C. MEYERS (3)

The grammar of mathematics includes the multiplication table, which, if learned now, will be learned with pleasure. This text, if followed, will lead the child to the acquisition of the skills appropriate to his age. It introduces division, practices identifying place value in five digit numbers, teaches about odd and even numbers, reviews addition and subtraction and introduces more difficult problems.

*Calculadder* is a drill program. It reinforces the child's knowledge of addition, subtraction, multiplication, and division facts and encourages the child to do the problems quickly.

READING, WRITING AND LANGUAGE ARTS — *The Writing Road to Reading* BY ROMALDA SPALDING (3), *Learning Language Arts Through Literature* (YELLOW BOOK) (3), *Honey for a Child's Heart* BY GLADYS HUNT (3), *Catholic Authors: 4-Sight Edition* BY THE BROTHERS OF MARY (10), AND GREENLEAF PRESS BOOKS (8), POETRY LIST

Once children are reading well, what they can do to improve their reading is read many good books. *The Writing Road to Reading* is not used at this point to teach reading, because that has been taught. It is an excellent text for reinforcing phonics rules and for spelling. There are other fine texts you might use to work on phonics and spelling; the text you use is not as important as the fact of doing it. These are subjects that improve with drill and can be learned well now. *Teaching Reading at Home* by Wanda Sanseri is a useful companion text to the *Writing Road.*

As I mentioned earlier, the *Writing Road to Reading* has a literature list at the back of the book that is quite good. *Honey for a Child's Heart, Catholic Authors,* and Greenleaf Press books all are other sources for reading material. It is still appropriate to spend some time reading more difficult books aloud to the child (or children; reading aloud is a great group activity). Listening to adult reading is a skill worth practicing. Fill the child's memory with stories of every kind.

The primary vehicle for writing in this year is the Bible history, but the Yellow Book of *Learning Language Arts Through Literature* has additional exercises that teach simple punctuation, dictionary use, and capitalization, as well as other appropriate skills. The rules learned here will be reinforced by application to the Bible stories.

Poems that we have used in third grade include "The Flag Goes By" by Henry Halcomb Bennett, "The Children's Hour," "The Village Blacksmith," "Christmas Bells," "The Tide Rises, The Tide Fails" by Henry Wadsworth Longfellow, "Casey at the Bat" by Ernest Lawrence Thayer, "Old Ironsides" by Oliver Wendell Holmes. The Preamble to the Constitution is another work to memorize.

SCIENCE — *Exploring God's World* WITH WORKBOOK (A BEKA) (5), BUTTERFLY GARDEN ACTIVITY KIT (INSECT LORE) (13 )

This is an excellent, simple, science text with well presented material. The workbook provides an opportunity to use reading skills to locate material, as well as reinforce concepts. Memorizing the classes of animals and placing animals into their class is one of the activities of this text that fits the idea of the "grammar" of science.

The Butterfly Garden kit allows the child to watch the entire life cycle of a butterfly. It is interesting and develops the child's ability to observe objectively and accurately.

HISTORY/GEOGRAPHY — *Our American Heritage* WITH WORKBOOK (A BEKA) (5), STATES AND CAPITALS FLASHCARDS (2)

The beginnings of our country will be studied through an acquaintance with prominent personalities of the time. This is an appropriate way to begin the study of history. Individual people are intelligible and accessible to small children, and are therefore easier to remember than isolated events. Such a study also teaches that individuals can and do have an impact on society and that individual action is therefore important. It leads to a sense of responsibility to the whole framework of society, which is an attitude young Catholics should have.

The workbook has exercises that should be used in moderation, but when used, do provide practice in a certain kind of comprehension skill.

If the child hasn't read all of the *Childhood of Famous Americans* series, now is a good time to do so.

A list of history dates should be memorized. This exercise employs the child's native abilities and is also an enormous help later on in establishing an historical perspective. There is a sample list at the end of this section.

The states and capitals should be reviewed if they were learned last year, and if not, they should be learned now.

Latin — *English from the Roots Up, Volume I* by Joegil Lundquist (3)

This is the first introduction to another language, the beginning of the study of Latin, with all the benefits I mentioned in "The Grammatical Stage." It is simple to use and effective.

Arts/Crafts — Craft kits (local craft store), or more crocheting, *Mommy, Its a Renoir* (Steps Four and Five) (3)

The crafts provide a directed forum for both large and fine motor control exercises. My children have enjoyed hammered metal pictures, building a birdhouse, making pencil holders, orange ball sachets, and so forth.

This level of *Mommy, It's a Renoir* involves learning the names of artists and famous pictures. It fits well with the idea of the "grammar" of the subject matter, and provides more exposure to beautiful works of art. As I suggested earlier, once the immediate goals of the art program are met, there are other uses of the pictures that will also encourage familiarity with these works.

Music — *Let's Learn Music # 2* (Hayes) (23), *The Music Masters* Series, Part # 3 (6)

*Let's Learn Music # 2* continues the study of music begun last year. The recorder text from last year could be continued or used for review. If your student has finished this text, the local music store will have some simple recorder music available.

Continue the study of the great works of music that has been pursued the previous two years. Discuss the music with your child, and the composer's life. Playing the pieces more than once helps fix the tunes in the imagination. It can be overdone, but some repetition is useful.

## TENTATIVE SCHEDULE FOR THIRD GRADE

| MON. | TUES. | WED. | THURS. | FRI. |
| --- | --- | --- | --- | --- |
| MATH | MATH | MATH | MATH | MATH |
| ENGLISH | ENGLISH | ENGLISH | ENGLISH | ENGLISH |
| RELIGION | RELIGION | RELIGION | RELIGION | RELIGION |
| MUSIC | HISTORY | SCIENCE | HISTORY | SCIENCE |
| ART | LATIN | | LATIN | |

EVENINGS — LITERATURE

## HISTORY DATES LIST FOR THIRD GRADE

| | |
| --- | --- |
| 1620 | "MAYFLOWER" LANDS PILGRIMS AT PLYMOUTH, MA. |
| 1776 | DECLARATION OF INDEPENDENCE |
| 1787 | U.S. CONSTITUTION |
| 1849 | CALIFORNIA GOLD RUSH |
| 1861 | CIVIL WAR BEGINS |
| 1865 | LEE SURRENDERS AT APPOMATTOX |
| 1914 | WORLD WAR I BEGINS IN EUROPE |
| 1918 | END OF WORLD WAR I |
| 1929 | STOCK MARKET CRASH — DEPRESSION BEGINS |
| 1941 | JAPAN ATTACKS PEARL HARBOR — U.S. ENTERS WORLD WAR II |
| 1945 | ATOMIC BOMB DROPPED ON HIROSHIMA; END OF WORLD WAR II |
| 1950 | KOREAN WAR BEGINS |
| 1957 | SPUTNIK |
| 1963 | VIETNAM WAR ESCALATES |
| 1969 | NEIL ARMSTRONG: FIRST MAN ON THE MOON |

# Fourth Grade Curriculum

**Sources for items followed by a number in parentheses may be found at the back of the book under the suppliers list.**

RELIGION — LIVES OF THE SAINTS (CORRELATED WITH HISTORY) (4), *St. Joseph's Baltimore Catechism No. I* (4), *Bible History* BY IGNATIUS SCHUSTER, D.D. (14), LATIN PRAYERS (SEE LIST)

During the first third of the year concentrate on reading various lives of the saints. Have your child choose, each week, a saint from the list that accompanies this section. This is a list of saints who lived during the period of history the child will be studying this year. The child will read about the saint and prepare an oral report which he should give to members of the family.

In addition to helping the child remember when the saint lived, the fact that the report is oral gives him a chance to inform others about something he knows which is important. It also exercises his communication skills. Another positive aspect of this activity is that the children enjoy it.

In the second third of the year the religion course will be concerned with Catholic doctrine. The child will use the third part of the Baltimore Catechism. His grasp of the material can be checked by having him do the exercises at the end of each chapter.

The questions and answers should be memorized. If you have more than one child in this class, or if you are willing to take a chance yourself, you can play spelling bee-like games to provide motivation and variety. You can also have the child supply the question for your answer, or give points and prizes for a certain number of correct answers. Always review previously learned material. It is better to move slowly through the text and learn the answers well, than to go quickly and forget them as soon as the chapter is finished. However, this material will be covered again, so if something is difficult or just doesn't seem to stick, don't worry too much. It will come up again.

In the third segment of the year, Bible History will be studied. The subject for writing this year will be in History and English. In Bible History the primary learning tool will be reading and conversing. Discuss the text with your child; have him summarize the chapter and then go over chapter questions with him.

Every Friday Religion class will be devoted to Latin prayers, learning to write as well as to say them. There is a list of prayers at the end of this section.

## MATHEMATICS — *Math 54* (SAXON) (3), *Calculadder* BY EDWIN C. MEYERS (3)

This text will introduce or review the basic fourth grade math skills. It has a cyclical approach, reviewing new material daily until it becomes second nature. *Calculadder* can be used to help the child do computations quickly.

## GRAMMAR AND COMPOSITION — *Learning Language Arts Through Literature* (ORANGE BOOK) (3), JOURNAL (BY YOUR CHILD)

Use this text, following its internal order. Special attention should be paid to the writing sections of the text. This provides practice in punctuation and capitalization, grammar and some variety in creative writing. The rules learned will be reinforced by application to the history summaries written at the end of each section of the history course.

The journal will be used as an extension of the text. When an exercise in the text is difficult and needs practice, or is particularly delightful, you can choose additional subjects for practice in the same kind of activity.

One of the exercises that my daughter found pleasant was turning poetry into prose. It seemed like a good thing to do since it required reading the poem closely, and because she thought it was fun, I would have her do one such exercise a month.

The journal may also be used to write descriptions of objects and special events, Latin prayers, and the current poem. It will provide penmanship practice and help with memorization as well as increase writing skills.

**SPELLING** — *The Writing Road to Reading* BY ROMALDA SPALDING (3), *Teaching Reading at Home* BY WANDA SANSERI (3)

If you have been using this text from the beginning, the phonics rules should be pretty familiar by now. The spelling list probably still contains words that are difficult. Use the spelling scale indicator in *Teaching Reading at Home* by Wanda Sanseri and determine the proper spelling level for your child. Start at that point in the text and continue to use the words through the year.

Also pay attention to accuracy in spelling in daily work. A list of words misspelled in daily work might be kept in the child's journal.

**LITERATURE** — (CORRELATED WITH HISTORY) LANDMARK BOOKS (8), *Books Children Love* BY ELIZABETH WILSON (3), GREENLEAF PRESS BOOKS (8), *In Review* (BETHLEHEM BOOKS) (9), *Let the Authors Speak* BY CAROLYN HATCHER (15), *Catholic Authors: 4-Sight Edition* BY THE BROTHERS OF MARY (10), *Honey for a Child's Heart* BY GLADYS HUNT (3)

Allow some time for reading literature each day, both silently and aloud. Discuss the stories with the children. *For the Children's Sake* by Susan Schaeffer Macaulay has good advice for how to discuss a text with your child.

I have included a list (at the end of this section) of suggested readings that fit with History for this year and are well written. Other texts can be found in the books I mention above.

**POETRY** — POEMS FROM AMERICAN AUTHORS (1)

Continue to encourage both memorization of enjoyable poems and recitation. When your child gives his oral report about the saint for the week you could also have him recite his poem. If he is working on a more difficult poem, you could have him recite it as far as he is able, or you could just wait until the whole thing is learned. I have included a list of poems that you may consider at the end of this section.

**SCIENCE** — *Understanding God's World* (5) OR HOW AND WHY BOOKS (1)

*Understanding God's World* is a good text and easy for the teacher to use. Just follow the internal order of the book. It is Christian, and

God's loving hand is seen in His creation in this book. However, it is difficult for some children, and rather technical.

An alternative is to purchase How and Why Books on subjects like earth science, astronomy, sound, chemistry, machines, and electricity. These books are informative and easy to read. They contain simple experiments that an older sibling could do with the student. Because they are accessible to the children the material is likely to be retained.

HISTORY — *Evangelization of the New World* BY JAMES R. LEEK (10), *Let the Authors Speak* BY CAROLYN HATCHER (15), BOOKS ABOUT EXPLORERS AND THE COLONIZATION OF THE NEW WORLD (3, 8, 9, 10, 17), *Turning Back the Pages of Time: A Guide to American History Through Literature* BY KATHY KELLER (15), *Pioneers and Patriots* BY FR. PHILIP FURLONG (7) OR SOME SIMILAR ALTERNATIVE TEXT

It is best to have some text to follow as an outline, and *Pioneers and Patriots* is a good Catholic text. It is, unfortunately, out of print. Protestant texts rarely have an objective view of the race for the New World. The best alternatives I have found are older secular texts, or more adult histories like *The Oxford History of the American People* by Samuel Eliot Morison. Such a text, however, will be for you to read and not for your child to read himself. Since the text is used as a springboard only, the quality of the text is not as essential here as it is in other areas.

Using the text you choose as an outline, read or have the child read the sections of the text dealing with the events and persons from the period of the early exploration of North America to the French and Indian War. Read each chapter, discuss it and then have the child read supplementary books that cover the same material in more depth. When those books, as many or as few as you choose, are read, have the child write a report, not a book report, but a report about the material covered. I have included a list of books for this period at the end of this section. Other texts can be found in the books I mention above.

*The Evangelization of the New World* contains important material about this period in history. It is an objective account of the Spanish colonization in Central, South and North America. It has original documents and additional information in the back of the text. The teacher's guide has good suggestions for discussion.

This way of doing history, where the textbook is an introduction to the information and not the primary vehicle, makes history come alive. Too often with a history text, the material seems dry and lifeless. The information is stored in the short term memory and promptly forgotten after the chapter test. The people I am acquainted with who know and love history, know the personalities and events as though they were currently alive. Writing about the outstanding people or events of each chapter will provide an opportunity to practice comprehension and composition skills.

This is a good time to start a timeline, which you can add to throughout the coming years. Or purchase a timeline that is already made but which can be referred to through the years. Timelines perform an important function because they tie together the studies of various disciplines chronologically.

Class time will vary from week to week depending on whether the chapter is being introduced, the material is being read or the summary being written. Keep the summaries throughout the year and at the end of the year there will be a very satisfying, abbreviated history by your child.

GEOGRAPHY — MAP SKILLS (2), U.S. MAP PUZZLE (10), *Where in the World?* GAME (10), U.S. OUTLINE MAPS (2)

First review the states and capitals. Then work on filling in the states and capitals from memory in an outline map. Your child should learn major rivers, mountains, and lakes and be able to place them correctly in the outline map.

Next use the map skills to learn map reading skills. This should be accompanied by reading actual maps.

The game *Where in the World?* can be used to fill in if there is extra time in the school year. Games are useful learning tools because they are relatively painless. Two good lists to learn at this point are largest states by area and largest states by population. They are included at the end of this chapter.

LATIN — *Latin Primer I* by MARTHA WILSON (3)

This continues the study begun last year of Latin and Greek roots commonly used in English. As you teach this course, which only takes minutes a day, you will find your own vocabulary and understanding of language increasing. One of the tremendous side benefits of homeschooling is that you get to learn the things you didn't learn when you were in school.

ART — *Mommy, It's a Renoir* (STEPS 6, 7, AND 8) (3), *Drawing Textbook* BY BRUCE MACINTYRE (3)

I recommend using the *Drawing Textbook* in the first half of the year. The introduction by Mr. MacIntyre is a convincing defense of the need for literacy in visual expression. Not everyone is an artist, but anyone can learn to draw recognizable objects.

Having learned some of the principles of drawing, the later steps of *Mommy, It's a Renoir* will have added interest. Steps 6, 7, and 8 are about schools of art, and the time when they flourished. When this information is mastered, other uses of the postcards are beneficial. One successful technique we have used is to have the child look at a particular picture, turn it over and then try to describe it so that it is visible to the listener. It is better if the listener has not just looked at the picture. Or the "listen-and-find" game, where one tries to pick out a picture from among many pictures by listening carefully to its description.

MUSIC — *Let's Learn Music # 3* (HAYES) (22), PLAY RECORDER, LISTEN TO CLASSICAL MUSIC, *Wee Sing America* (3)

*Let's Learn Music # 3* continues the study of music begun in second grade. Simple recorder music continues to be used for application of principles.

Continue the study of the great works of music that has been pursued in the previous years. If you have worked your way through *The Music Masters* Series, now is the time to become familiar with particular pieces of music. Pick some of your favorites from the tapes and play them often enough so that the child recognizes them. Then you can play recognition games, asking your child which piece of music this is and who wrote it. Recognition is a pleasure for everyone and is especially enjoyable in this grammatical period of education.

*Wee Sing America* teaches songs that have been important in the history of our country, so it is appropriate to use it as the history of our country is studied.

## TENTATIVE SCHEDULE FOR FOURTH GRADE

| Mon. | Tues. | Wed. | Thurs. | Fri. |
|------|-------|------|--------|------|
| MATH | MATH | MATH | MATH | MATH |
| ENGLISH | ENGLISH | ENGLISH | ENGLISH | ENGLISH |
| GEOGRAPHY | RELIGION | HISTORY | RELIGION | GEOGRAPHY |
| SCIENCE | ART | MUSIC | LITERATURE | LATIN PRAYERS |

MEMORIZATION PRACTICE IN THE VARIOUS SUBJECTS EVERY DAY

# Grade Four Resource Lists

## Saint List for Fourth Grade Religion

St. Kateri Tekawitha
St. Rose of Lima
Father Serra
St. Isaac Jogues
St. Phillip Neri
St. Alphonsus Ligouri
St. John Baptiste De La Salle
St. Elizabeth Ann Seton
St. John Neumann
St. John Vianney
  (The Cure d'Ars)
St. John Bosco
Pope St. Pius X

St. Theresa of Lisieux
St. Angela Merici
St. Ignatius Loyola
St. Charles Borromeo
St. Francis Xavier
St. Peter Canisius
St. Francis de Sales
St. Vincent de Paul
St. Paul of the Cross
St. Bernadette
St. Dominic Savio

## Latin Prayers

*Pater Noster* (Our Father)

Pater Noster, qui es in caelis, sanctificetur nomen tuum, adveniat regnum tuum, fiat voluntas tua, sicut in caelo et in terra. Panem nostrum quotidianum da nobis hodie, et dimitte nobis debita nostra sicut et nos dimittimus debitoribus nostris, et ne nos inducas in tentationem, sed libera nos a malo. Amen.

*Ave Maria* (Hail Mary)

Ave Maria, gratia plena, dominus tecum, benedicta tu in mulieribus, et benedictus fructus ventris tui, Jesus. Sancta Maria, Mater Dei, ora pro nobis peccatoribus nunc et in hora mortis nostrae. Amen.

*Gloria* (Glory Be)

Gloria Patri, et Filio, et Spiritui Sancto, sicut erat in principio, et nunc et semper et in saecula saeculorum. Amen.

*Gratia* (Grace before meals)

Benedic, Domine, nos, et haec tua dona, quae de tua largitate sumus sumpturi, per Christum Dominum nostrum. Amen. Animae omnium fidelium defunctorum per misericordiam Dei requiescant in pace. Amen.

# GEOGRAPHY LIST FOR FOURTH GRADE— LARGEST STATES

## LARGEST STATES BY AREA

| | |
|---|---|
| ALASKA | 590,000 SQ. MILES |
| TEXAS | 270,000 SQ. MILES (HALF OF ALASKA) |
| CALIFORNIA | 160,000 SQ. MILES (A LITTLE MORE THAN HALF OF TEXAS) |
| MONTANA | 150,000 SQ. MILES |

OTHERS OVER 100,000 SQ. MILES:

| | |
|---|---|
| NEW MEXICO | (120,000) |
| ARIZONA | (114,000) |
| NEVADA | (110,000) |
| COLORADO | (104,000) |

## LARGEST STATES BY POPULATION (1990 CENSUS)

| | | |
|---|---|---|
| CALIFORNIA | 30 MILLION | 54 ELECTORAL VOTES |
| NEW YORK | 18 MILLION | 33 ELECTORAL VOTES |
| TEXAS | 17 MILLION | 32 ELECTORAL VOTES |
| FLORIDA | 13 MILLION | 25 ELECTORAL VOTES |
| PENNSYLVANIA | 12 MILLION | 23 ELECTORAL VOTES |
| ILLINOIS | 11 MILLION | 22 ELECTORAL VOTES |
| OHIO | 11 MILLION | 21 ELECTORAL VOTES |
| MICHIGAN | 9 MILLION | 8 ELECTORAL VOTES |

# HISTORY READING LIST FOR FOURTH GRADE— THE AGE OF EXPLORATION

Used as supplements to the first half of *Pioneers and Patriots* by Fr. Philip Furlong.

An "L" after the author's name indicates that the library or used book sources will be your best bet for securing this title, "IP" indicates that the book is currently in print, "*" indicates an especially enjoyable book. If a book belongs to an identifiable series I will indicate that by using one of the following abbreviations: VB — Vision Book (Catholic), AMB — American Background Book (Catholic), LKB — Landmark Book (Christian orientation), SB — Signature Book, NSB — North Star Book, CL — Clarion Book (Catholic).

| | | |
|---|---|---|
| *The Vikings* | ELIZABETH JANEWAY | IP,* LKB |
| *The Black Fox of Lorne* | MARGUERITE DE ANGELI | L,* |
| *Door to the North* | ELIZABETH COATSWORTH | L,* |
| *Leif Ericson* | WILLIAM STEELE | L,* |
| *He Went with Marco Polo* | LOUISE ANDREWS KENT | L,* |
| *He Went with Vasco de Gama* | LOUISE ANDREWS KENT | L,* |
| *Christopher Columbus* | NINA BROWN BAKER | L, SB |
| *The Voyage of Christopher Columbus* | ARMSTRONG SPERRY | L, LKB |
| *Columbus* | INGRI AND EDGAR D'AULAIRE | IP,* |
| *Columbus and the New World* | AUGUST DERLETH | L,* VB |
| *Queen Elizabeth and the Spanish Armada* | FRANCES WINWAR | L, LKB |
| *The Evangelization of the New World* | STEPHEN LEEK | IP,* |
| *New Found World* | KATHERINE B. SHIPPEN | L |
| *Cortes of Mexico* | RONALD SYME | L,* |
| *Balboa Discovers the Pacific* | JEANNETTE MIRSKY | L,* |
| *Ferdinand Magellan* | RONALD WELCH | L,* |
| *Ship's Boy with Magellan* | MILTON LOMOSK | L,* |
| *Ferdinand Magellan* | SEYMOUR POND | L, LKB |
| *Henry Hudson, Captain of Ice Bound Seas* | CARL CARMER | L |
| *Champlain of the St. Lawrence* | RONALD SYME | L,* |
| *The Hudson Bay Company* | RICHARD MORENUS | L, LKB |
| *The First Northwest Passage* | WALTER O'MEARA | L, NSB |
| *Peter Stuyvesant of Old New York* | ANNA AND RUSSEL CROUSE | L, LKB |
| *Jamestown* | JAMES E. KNIGHT | IP |

| | | |
|---|---|---|
| *The Landing of the Pilgrims* | JAMES DAUGHERTY | IP,* LKB |
| *Cartier Sails the St. Lawrence* | ESTHER AVERILL | L |
| *I Sailed on the Mayflower* | PILKINGTON | IP |
| *Sailing the Seven Seas* | MARY CHASE | L, NSB |
| *Clipper Ship Days* | JOHN JENNINGS | L, LKB |
| *Captain Cook Explores the South Seas* | ARMSTRONG SPERRY | L |
| *Fear in the Forest* | CATEAU DE LEEUW | L,* |
| *The French are Coming* | WILMA HAYS | L, LKB |
| *Rogers' Rangers, The French and Indian War* | BRADFORD SMITH | L |
| *Ticonderoga, The Story of a Fort* | BRUCE LANCASTER | L, NSB |
| *St. Isaac and the Indians* | MILTON LOMASK | IP,* VB |
| *Cross Among the Tomahawks* | MILTON LOMASK | L,* CL |
| *Sing in the Dark* | MAUDE THOMAS | L,* |
| *Indian Captive* | LOIS LENSKI | L,* |
| *Captured by the Mohawks* | STERLING NORTH | L,* |
| *Battle for the Rock* | JOSEPH SCHULL | L,* |
| *De Tonti Of the Iron Hand* | ANN HEAGNEY | L,* AMB |
| *The Explorations of Pere Marquette* | JIM KJELGAARD | L,* LKM |
| *Father Marquette and the Great River* | AUGUST DERLETH | L,* VB |
| *Crusaders of the Great River* | FR. WILLIAM DOTY | L,* |
| *The Cross in the West* | MARK BOESCH | L,* VB |
| *Fr. Junipero Serra* | IVY BOLTON | L,* |
| *Father Kino, Priest to the Pimas* | ANN CLARK | L,* VB |
| *Padre Kino* | JACK STEFFAN | L,* AMB |

# POETRY LIST FOR FOURTH GRADE

| | |
|---|---|
| "HIAWATHA'S CHILDHOOD" FROM "THE SONG OF HIAWATHA," | HENRY WADSWORTH LONGFELLOW |
| "COLUMBUS" | JOAQUIN MILLER |

| | |
|---|---|
| "America for Me" | Henry Van Dyke |
| "Sea Fever" | John Masefield |
| "Christmas Everywhere" | Phillip Brooks |
| "The Duel" | Eugene Field |
| "The Fool's Prayer" | Edward Sill |
| "The Bells" | Edgar Allan Poe |
| "Spring" | Alfred Lord Tennyson |
| "Requiem" | Robert Louis Stevenson |
| "Christopher Columbus" | Rosemary and Stephen Vincent Benet |
| "Hernando De Soto" | Rosemary and Stephen Vincent Benet |
| "Pocahontas" | Rosemary and Stephen Vincent Benet |
| "Captain Kidd" | Rosemary and Stephen Vincent Benet |
| "George Washington" | Rosemary and Stephen Vincent Benet |

# Fifth Grade Curriculum

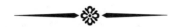

**Sources for items followed by a number in parentheses may be found at the back of the book under the suppliers list.**

RELIGION — *Faith and Life Catechism* FOR GRADE 5 *(Credo: I Believe)* (4), *St. Joseph's Baltimore Catechism No. 2* (4)

Read and discuss all 30 chapters in the Catechism. This is an excellent treatment of the basic truths of our faith. The questions and answers in the text are from the Catechism of St. Pius X and are less distilled than the *Baltimore Catechism*. The doctrine presented is the same, but the articulation of that doctrine is more complex and therefore more difficult for little children. When I use this book I substitute the *Baltimore Catechism* questions for those in the text.

MATHEMATICS — *Math 65* (SAXON) (3)

*Math 65* is a standard textbook for this grade level, so the appropriate concepts for this stage of learning will be covered. Once again the spiral approach to teaching makes this a first-rate text. The child never forgets a concept once learned because he practices it every day. Complete the text over the course of the year, with periodic quizzes and tests to check on progress.

GRAMMAR AND COMPOSITION — *Learning Language Arts Through Literature* (TAN BOOK) (3), *Harvey's Grammar* (3) OR *Voyages in English Grade 5* (12)

In our house the subject of writing concentration varies in the fifth grade. The child who really enjoyed last year's history writing program continues with it, but for those who are not as delighted with writing summaries we use the Tan Book as the primary writing source. This text emphasizes different kinds of writing with daily practice and exercises. There is practice in writing letters, invitations, original prose and poetry. There are also numerous opportunities for writing from dictation, which is a very beneficial practice.

It requires concentration on spelling, punctuation and styles of writing.

Grammar will be begun as a separate study this year. *Harvey's Grammar* is thorough and has good streamlined exercises. It is an excellent text. *The Voyages in English* is an easier text, and does introduce the basic parts of speech. In either case, grammar is a subject that requires teacher interaction for mastery. It is possible to do the exercises without understanding, by simply following the examples. The teacher needs to be involved so that the pupil has to concentrate and think about not only the present concept but also the previously learned material. Grammar, composition, spelling, literature, and poetry are all directed to giving the child a practical and theoretical knowledge of language which will enable him to read, write, and think well.

## SPELLING — *The Writing Road to Reading* BY ROMALDA SPALDING (3)

Though you have been using this text for some time and the phonics rules are quite familiar, the spelling list probably still contains words that are difficult. If it does not, concentrate on spelling well in daily work but don't have a separate text for spelling. Use the spelling scale indicator in *Teaching Reading at Home* by Wanda Sanseri to help determine whether your child will profit by continued work with this text.

In any case pay particular attention to accurate spelling in daily work. A list of daily misspellings might be kept in a notebook.

## LITERATURE — (CORRELATED WITH HISTORY) LANDMARK BOOKS (8), *Books Children Love* BY ELIZABETH WILSON (3), GREENLEAF PRESS BOOKS (8), *Catholic Authors: 4-Sight Edition* BY THE BROTHERS OF MARY (10), *Let the Authors Speak* BY CAROLYN HATCHER (15)

As you did last year, allow some time for reading literature each day. Discuss the stories with the children. Once again I would like to point out that *For the Children's Sake* by Susan Schaeffer Macaulay has good advice for how to discuss a text with your child.

Though discussing some of your child's reading with him is both rewarding and important (not to mention occasionally hilarious), not all texts lend themselves equally to discussion. Don't feel that every book your child reads has to be talked over. Further, each child should be able to do some reading with "no strings attached," just for fun, without any end in view other than enjoyment. The book list I have included has works on it that my own children have found delightful; all of these are marked with an asterisk.

I have included a list (at the end of this section) of suggested readings that fit with history for this year and are well written. Other texts can be found in the books I mention above.

POETRY — POEMS FROM AMERICAN AUTHORS (1)

Continue to encourage both memorization of enjoyable poems and recitation. This year you might include some longer speeches. It is more of a challenge to memorize prose than poetry, and is correspondingly strengthening to the imagination and retentive powers.

I have included a list of poems and prose selections that you may consider at the end of this section.

SCIENCE — *Concepts and Challenges in Science* (A) BY ALAN WINKLER, LEONARD BERNSTEIN, MARLTIN SCHACHTER AND STANLEY WOLFE (PUBLISHED BY GLOBE) (25)

*Concepts and Challenges* contains an excellent presentation of the basic concepts of biology, physics, chemistry and earth science at this level. There are simple experiments which may be done as time permits. This text is not difficult and does not include large amounts of detail. But it does fit well with the aim of this curriculum, because it concentrates on basic formation and not on an accumulation of complex data. Have the child do one chapter each day to finish the book easily by the end of the year.

HISTORY — BOOKS ABOUT THE REVOLUTIONARY WAR PERIOD THROUGH THE CIVIL WAR (8), YOUR TEXT BOOK (SEE LAST YEAR), *Let the Authors Speak* BY CAROLYN HATCHER (15), *Turning Back the Pages of Time: A Guide to American History Through Literature* BY KATHY KELLER (15)

Using the text you choose as an outline, read — or have your child read — the sections of the text dealing with the events and persons from the period of the Revolutionary War through the Civil War. Read each chapter, discuss it and then have the child read supplementary books that cover the same material in more depth. When

61

those books, as many or as few as you choose, are read, have the child write a report if this is the area you have chosen for writing practice. Otherwise, discuss the chapter in the light of the books covered. I have included a list of books for this period at the end of this section. Other texts can be found in the books I mention above.

As I mentioned in the fourth grade curriculum, this way of doing history, where the textbook simply introduces the information and is not the primary vehicle, makes history more interesting and memorable. Dates are good to memorize in conjunction with such a study because they are hooks to hang the information on.

Have your child keep track of important dates as they come up in the reading material. This can be a list for memory work.

Class time will vary from week to week depending on whether the chapter is being introduced, the material is being read or discussed.

## GEOGRAPHY — MAP STUDY WITH AN ATLAS (2)

We want our children to become proficient at locating cities and countries on a map. This requires attention to detail, so after reviewing the states and capitals, I recommend using an atlas and giving the student a small photocopied piece of map which contains an identifying feature (well-known city or mountain range). Cut a circle out of a piece of paper and place the paper on the map, with the cut-out positioned over the identifying feature. Then photocopy it. Instruct your child to find the map from which the piece is taken and answer questions about it. Ask him what continent the landmark is on, what country it is in, and what the latitude and longitude of the identifying feature is. (This is a homemade alternative to *Geo-Safari* or *Where in the World?*. The advantage it has is that it works with real maps, which the child is able to do, but which most programs do not use. The disadvantage, obviously, is that it is more work for you.)

I have included a good list to learn at this point at the end of this section. It is the continents and their square mileage, with the highest point in each continent and the same information about the island groups.

LATIN — *Latin Primer, Book II* BY MARTHA WILSON (3)

This is my favorite Latin text because it is perfect for teaching the language at this stage. The child memorizes many vocabulary words and learns the paradigms (-o, -s, -t, -mus, -tis, -nt). It is easy to use, does not require lots of time and it works. The children learn these fundamental tools and practice some translation skills.

ART — *Great Painters* BY PIERO VENTURA (1), *Drawing Textbook* BY BRUCE MACINTYRE (3)

I recommend using the *Drawing Textbook* again in the first half of the year. The child may review or pick up where he left off last year. Practice is necessary for literacy in visual expression. Though not every one is an artist, anyone can learn, with practice, to draw recognizable objects.

Having reviewed some of the principles of drawing, and with the background the child has acquired with *Mommy, Its a Renoir, Great Painters* will have added interest. The text talks about the various artists and their histories. The schools of art, and the time when they flourished, are discussed.

MUSIC — *Music Reading* BY LORETTA MITCHELL (15), PLAY RECORDER, LISTEN TO CLASSICAL MUSIC

*Music Reading* continues the theoretical study of music. It is a program that teaches music using music. It has singing as well as instrumental playing. It is slow and methodical so that even a parent with no musical training can use it confidently. It does require a piano, keyboard or chromatic bells and rhythm sticks.

Continue the study of the great works of music that has been pursued in the previous years. Work on familiarity with particular pieces of music. Pick some of your favorites and play them often enough so that the child recognizes them. Then you can play recognition games, asking your child which piece of music this is and who wrote it. Recognition is a pleasure for everyone and is especially enjoyable in this grammatical period of education.

## TENTATIVE SCHEDULE FOR FIFTH GRADE

| MON. | TUES. | WED. | THUR. | FRI. |
|---|---|---|---|---|
| MATH | MATH | MATH | MATH | MATH |
| ENGLISH | ENGLISH | ENGLISH | ENGLISH | HISTORY |
| RELIGION | RELIGION | RELIGION | RELIGION | ART |
| SCIENCE | SCIENCE | SCIENCE | SCIENCE | |
| MUSIC | GEOGRAPHY | HISTORY | HISTORY | |
| LATIN | LATIN | LATIN | LATIN | |

MEMORIZATION PRACTICE IN THE VARIOUS SUBJECTS EVERY DAY

# Grade Five Resource Lists

## History Reading List for Grade Five— The Beginning of the United States

Used as supplements to the second half of *Pioneers and Patriots* by Fr. Philip Furlong.

An "L" after the author's name indicates that the library or used book sources will be your best bet for securing this title, "IP" indicates that the book is currently in print, "*" indicates an especially enjoyable book. If a book belongs to an identifiable series I will indicate that by using one of the following abbreviations: VB — Vision Book (Catholic), AMB — American Background Book (Catholic), LKB — Landmark Book (Christian orientation), SB — Signature Book, NSB — North Star Book, WWTB — We Were There Books.

| | | |
|---|---|---|
| *William Penn, Quaker Hero* | Hildegarde Dolson | L , LKB |
| *Roger Williams, Defender of Freedom* | Cecile Edwards | L |
| *Builders of Catholic America* | Albert Nevins, M.M. | IP |
| *George Washington's World* | Genevieve Foster | L, * |
| *Arrow Book of Presidents* | Sturges Cary | L |
| American Heritage *Book of the Presidents* (in many volumes) | | L |
| *The Golden Book of America* | Irwin Shapiro | L |
| *Landmark History* (two volumes) | Daniel J. Boorstin | IP, * |
| *The Witch of Blackbird Pond* (older children) | Elizabeth George Speare | IP, * |
| *Sarah Morton's Day* | Kate Waters | IP, * |
| *Ben Franklin of Old Philadelphia* | Margaret Cousins | IP, * LKB |
| *Ben and Me* | Robert Lawson | IP, * |
| *Mr. Revere and I* | Robert Lawson | IP, * |
| *The American Revolution* | Bruce Bliven, Jr. | IP, LKB |

| | | |
|---|---|---|
| John Carroll, Bishop and Patriot | MILTON LOMASK | L, * VB |
| Paul Revere and the Minute Men | DOROTHY CANFIELD FISHER | L, * LKB |
| Drums | JAMES BOYD | L |
| Silver for General Washington | ENID MEADOWCROFT | L,* |
| Johnny Tremain | ESTHER FORBES | IP, * |
| Cavalry Hero, Casimir Pulaski | DOROTHY ADAMS | L, * AMB |
| Birth of the Constitution | EDMUND LINDOP | IP |
| Our Independence and the Constitution | DOROTHY CANFIELD FISHER | IP, * LKB |
| John Paul Jones, Fighting Sailor | ARMSTRONG SPERRY | L, LKB |
| A Boy Sailor with John Paul Jones | H.C. THOMAS | L, * |
| The Story of John Paul Jones | IRIS VINTON | L |
| Old Ironsides | HARRY HANSEN | L, LKB |
| Marquis De Lafayette | HODDING CARTER | L, LKB |
| Early American | MILDRED PACE | L |
| A Spy in Old West Point | ANNE EMERY | L |
| The West Point Story | COLONEL RED REEDER AND NARDI REEDER CAMPION | L, LKB |
| The Swamp Fox of the Revolution | STEWART H. HOLBROOK | L, * LKB |
| The Far Frontier | WILLIAM STEELE | L |
| Daniel Boone, Opening of the Wilderness | JOHN BROWN | L, LKB |
| General Brock and Niagara Falls | SAMUEL ADAMS | L, LKB |
| Traders and Trappers of the Far West | JAMES DAUGHERTY | L, LKB |
| Davy Crockett | CONTANCE ROURKE | L |
| The Louisiana Purchase | ROBERT TALLANT | L, LKB |
| Lafayette, Friend of America | ALBERTA GRAHAM | L |

| | | |
|---|---|---|
| *The Battle for New Orleans* | F. Van Wyck Mason | L, NSB |
| *The Pirate Lafitte and the Battle of New Orleans* | Robert Tallant | L, LKB |
| *Robert Fulton and the Steamboat* | Ralph Hill | L, LKB |
| *Wyatt Earp* | Stewart H. Holbrook | L, LKB |
| *Buffalo Bill's Great Wild West Show* | Walter Havighurst | L, LKB |
| *Up the Trail fom Texas* | J. Frank Dobie | L, LKB |
| *Trail Blazer of the Seas* | Jean Lee Latham | L, * |
| *Simon Brute and the Western Adventure* | Elizabeth Bartelme | L, * AMB |
| *Erie Canal* | Samuel Adams | L, LKB |
| *Kit Carson and the Wild Frontier* | Ralph Moody | L, * LKB |
| *War Chief of the Seminoles* | May McNeer | L, LKB |
| *We Were Then at the Klondike Gold Rush* | Benjamin Appel | L, WWTB |
| *The Alaska Gold Rush* | May McNeer | L, LKB |
| *Dolly Madison* | Jane Mayer | L, LKB |
| *Abraham Lincoln's World* | Genevieve Foster | L, * |
| *Robert E. Lee and the Road Of Honor* | Hodding Carter | L, LKB |
| *By Secret Railway* | Enid Meadowcroft | L, * |
| *Lincoln and Douglas, The Years of Decision* | Regina Kelly | L, LKB |
| *Gettysburg* | MacKinlay Kantor | IP, LKB |
| *Abe Lincoln: Log Cabin to White House* | Sterling North | IP, LKB |
| *We Were There at the Battle of Gettysburg* | Alida Malkus | L, WWTB |
| *Rifles for Watie* | Harold Keith | IP, * |
| *Amos Fortune, Free Man* | Elizabeth Yates | IP, * |
| *Across Five Aprils* | Irene Hunt | IP, * |
| *The Story of Andrew Jackson* | Enid Meadowcroft | L, SB |
| *The Story of Clara Barton* | Olive Price | L, SB |
| *Stonewall Jackson* | Jonathan Daniels | L, LKB |
| *William Gaston, Fighter for Justice* | Eva Betz | L, * AMB |

| | | |
|---|---|---|
| *Chaplain in Gray* | H.J. HEAGNEY | L, * AMB |
| *Lee and Grant at Appomattox* | MACKINLAY KANTOR | L, LKB |
| *Man Of the Monitor* | JEAN LEE LATHAM | L, * |
| *The Birth of Texas* | WILLIAM JOHNSON | L, NSB |
| *Sam Houston, The Tallest Texan* | WILLIAM JOHNSON | L, LKB |
| *Sam Houston* | BOOTH MOONEY | L |
| *We Were There at the Oklahoma Land Run* | JIM KJELGAARD | L, WWTB |
| *The Buffalo Knife* | WILLIAM O. STEELE | IP, * |
| *James Bowie* | SHANNON GARST | L |
| *We Were There at the Driving of the Golden Spike* | DAVID SHEPHERD | L, WWTB |
| *The Oregon Trail* | FRANCIS PARKMAN | IP, * |
| *We Were There on the Oregon Trail* | WILLIAM O. STEELE | L, WWTB |
| *Custer's Last Stand* | QUENTIN REYNOLD | L, LKB |
| *The Story of General Custer* | MARGARET LEIGHTON | L, SB |
| *The Story of Crazy Horse* | ENID MEADOWCROFT | L, SB |
| *The Story of Geronimo* | JIM KJELGAARD | L, * SB |
| *Heroines of the Early West* | NANCY ROSS | L, LKB |
| *Caddie Woodlawn* | CAROL RYRIE BRINK | IP, * |
| *The Little House* BOOKS | LAURA INGALLS WILDER | IP, * |
| *The Pioneers Go West* | GEORGE STEWART | IP, LKB |
| *Mr. Bell Invents the Telephone* | KATHERINE SHIPPEN | L, LKB |
| *To California by Covered Wagon* | GEORGE STEWART | L, LKB |
| *Broken Hand Fitzpatrick* | SHANNON GARST | L |
| *Young Man in a Hurry* | JEAN LEE LATHAM | L, * |
| *Sons of the Big Muddy* | WILBUR GRANBERG | L |
| *A First Steamboat on the Mississippi* | STERLING NORTH | L, NSB |
| *The Story of Thomas Alva Edison* | MARGARET COUSINS | IP, LKB |
| *Young Thomas Edison* | STERLING NORTH | L, SB |
| *The Conquest of the North and South Poles* | RUSSELL OWEN | L, LKB |
| *Teddy Roosevelt and the Rough Riders* | HENRY CASTOR | L, LKB |

## POETRY LIST AND OTHER WORKS TO MEMORIZE FOR FIFTH GRADE

| | |
|---|---|
| "GEORGE WASHINGTON" | ROSEMARY AND STEPHEN VINCENT BENET |
| "JOHN ADAMS" | ROSEMARY AND STEPHEN VINCENT BENET |
| "BENJAMIN FRANKLIN" | ROSEMARY AND STEPHEN VINCENT BENET |
| "LEWIS AND CLARK" | ROSEMARY AND STEPHEN VINCENT BENET |
| "JOHN QUINCY ADAMS" | ROSEMARY AND STEPHEN VINCENT BENET |
| "JOHN PAUL JONES" | ROSEMARY AND STEPHEN VINCENT BENET |
| "THE STAR SPANGLED BANNER" | FRANCIS SCOTT KEY |
| "PAUL REVERE'S RIDE" | HENRY WADSWORTH LONGFELLOW |
| "THE WAR INEVITABLE, MARCH, 1775" | PATRICK HENRY |
| "THE CONCORD HYMN" | RALPH WALDO EMERSON |
| "O CAPTAIN! MY CAPTAIN!" | WALT WHITMAN |
| "SHERIDAN'S RIDE" | THOMAS BUCHANAN READ |
| "THE DESTRUCTION OF SENNECHARIB" | LORD BYRON |
| "SOLITUDE" | ELLA WHEELER WILCOX |
| "THE SPIDER AND THE FLY" | MARY HOWITT |
| "THE RIDE OF COLIN GRAVES" | J.B. O'REILLY |
| "HOW THEY BROUGHT THE GOOD NEWS FROM GHENT TO AIX" | ROBERT BROWNING |
| *"Jesu dulcis memoria"* | ST. BERNARD OF CLAIRVAUX (ENGLISH TRANSLATION G.M.HOPKINS) |

OTHER WORKS
    "WASHINGTON'S ADDRESS TO HIS TROOPS"
    "WASHINGTON ON HIS APPOINTMENT AS COMMANDER-IN-CHIEF "

69

# Geography List for Fifth Grade— Continents and Island Groups Listed

## Continents

| Continent | Area (sq. miles) | Est. population (Jan. 1987) | Highest Point (ft.) |
|---|---|---|---|
| 1 North America | 9,400,000 | 407,200,000 | Mt. McKinley, United States 20,320 |
| 2 South America | 6,900,000 | 276,700,000 | Cerro Aconcagua, Argentina 22,831 |
| 3 Europe | 3,800,000 | 680,100,000 | Mt. Elbrus, Russia 18,510 |
| 4 Asia | 17,300,000 | 2,985,300,000 | Mt. Everest, China, Nepal 29,028 |
| 5 Africa | 11,700,000 | 600,600,000 | Mt. Kilimanjaro, Tanzania 19,340 |
| 6 Australia | 2,966,153 | 16,065,000 | Mt. Kosciusko, N. South Wales 7,310 |
| 7 Antarctica | 5,400,000 | | Vinson Massif 16,864 |

## Island Groups

| Continent | Area (sq. miles) | Est. population (Jan. 1987) | Highest Point (ft.) |
|---|---|---|---|
| 8 Oceania (includes Indian, Pacific and Atlantic Oceans) | 333,847 | 9,035,000 | Mt. Wilhelm, Pap. New Guin. 14,793 |

## Entire World

| Area (sq. miles) | Est. population (Jan. 1987) |
|---|---|
| 57,800,000 | 4,975,000,000 |

# Sixth Grade Curriculum

**Sources for items followed by a number in parentheses may be found at the back of the book under the suppliers list.**

RELIGION — NEW TESTAMENT (*Mark* AND *Luke*), *Baltimore Catechism No. 2* (4)

In addition to the study of doctrine there should be readings that inspire and stir the heart. Attentive reading of the *Gospels* will supply this need. It will also encourage familiarity with the New Testament, the heart of our written heritage of Faith.

*St. Mark's Gospel* will be discussed with the child. Questions for each chapter are included at the end of this section. I recommend doing *Mark's Gospel* first and then *St. Luke*. Both for the sake of variety and because it is good in itself, have the child write a short synopsis of every chapter in the *Gospel of St. Luke*. Have him work on producing an account that is accurate, interesting, unified, and coherent. With both *Gospels* include some oral reading of the text and concentrate on smoothness and appropriateness of expression.

This *Catechism*, the *No. 2*, is the next level of the expression of the doctrine of the Church. It is the same material but formulated in a slightly more complex manner than in the previous text. Use the last third of the year for the first section of the *Catechism*. If there is an interest on the child's part for a more in-depth understanding of the chapters use *The Baltimore Catechism Explained* by Fr. Thomas L. Kincaid (14).

MATHEMATICS — *Math 76* (SAXON) (3)

Mathematics is important for further learning because it is a kind of paradigm of knowledge and truth. It is also important in the practical needs of life. In general at this stage, we aim for facility in computation and the understanding of principles and proofs that is appropriate at this level of education. Use the text five days a week, following the internal order.

**GRAMMAR AND COMPOSITION** — *Voyages in English 6* (12) OR *Harvey's Grammar* (3), PAPERS IN HISTORY

*The Voyages in English* text is a very good, thorough treatment of English grammar. The text contains both writing and grammar exercises, but the grammar by itself will take the full year to go through carefully. Since there will be written assignments in both Religion and History it is not necessary to use the writing portion of the text. *Harvey's Grammar* is also an excellent text. If you used it in fifth grade, you will already have it and may want to keep on with it. In this case review the parts of speech you have already covered before you continue. In either case have your student diagram sentences.

The grammar of language is an important educational tool for the child over the next three years. Students can master this discipline. They see that it is possible to learn in such a way that the mind grasps the subject and is satisfied. Additionally, diagramming provides wonderful analytic practice. Attention must be paid to every part of the sentence and a classification of each part is necessary. This is one of the skills that will lead into the next stage of the Trivium, the Dialectic, where clearsighted analysis must be made of the parts of arguments.

**SPELLING** — *The Writing Road to Reading* BY ROMALDA SPALDING (3) AND CLOSE ATTENTION TO DAILY WORK

This is the last year we will use *The Writing Road to Reading*. The phonics rules should be well known by now, and the spelling lists familiar. Primary attention in spelling will be to daily work, particularly in Religion and History. Review the phonics rules as necessary, and use the latter parts of the spelling list. You may use the spelling scale in *Teaching Reading at Home* by Wanda Sanseri to determine the proper spelling level.

**LITERATURE** — (CORRELATED WITH HISTORY) LANDMARK BOOKS (8), *Books Children Love* BY ELIZABETH WILSON (3), GREENLEAF PRESS BOOKS (8), *In Review* (9), ALSO *Catholic Author* LISTS (10), *Honey for a Child's Heart* LISTS BY GLADYS HUNT (3), *Let the Authors Speak* BY CAROLYN HATCHER (15)

It is crucial to fill the imagination of children with rich and varied images. Careful selection of poetry, literature and Scripture readings will do this and will contribute to a lifetime of thoughtful, serious, intelligent reading. I have included two lists at the end of this section that offer suggestions for literature and history selections. There is also a poetry list. Other texts can be found in the books I mention above.

As I mentioned earlier, discussing some of your child's reading with him is both rewarding and important. At the same time, each child should be able to do some reading just for fun, without any end in view other than enjoyment. This will encourage life-long reading. Find out what kinds of books appeal to your child and spend some time collecting more of that particular kind of book. Put them in an accessible place and make sure there is some reading time each day. The history readings for this year are fewer than in other years, so I really encourage my children to read fictional works during this year. The book list I have included has works on it that both I and my children have found delightful.

## POETRY — SEE LIST

Reading and memorizing beautiful and evocative English will be used to improve knowledge of rhetorical patterns, as well as contribute to a well furnished imagination. Work on a poem every day and when it has been memorized copy it into a notebook. At the end of the year you will have a personalized poetry anthology.

## SCIENCE — TOPS *Magnetism* AND *Electricity* UNITS (15)

These units are largely a hands-on, self-teaching approach to the subjects. They encourage the child to explore and understand the principles of magnetism and electricity by the application of logical thinking skills to a restricted matter. They are relatively easy to use and allow opportunities for thoughtful analysis that is commensurate with the child's ability.

## HISTORY — BOOKS ABOUT ANCIENT CIVILIZATIONS (8,9), *The Old World and America* BY FR. PHILIP FURLONG (14), *Let the Authors Speak* BY CAROLYN HATCHER (15)

*The Old World and America* is an excellent text. It is interesting, has good exercises and a Catholic perspective. This is the text I recommend using for the next three years, while studying ancient civilizations and the middle ages.

This course concentrates on the earliest cultures, the personalities and events in the early Egyptian, Assyrian, Babylonian, and Hebrew civilizations. A short list of supplementary readings is included at the end of this section. Other texts can be found in the books I mention above.

Young children lack the experience to form judgments about political issues. History provides for them a storehouse of data and human understanding, as well as being interesting in its own right. Learning about these peoples and nations is the beginning of political prudence, right judgment and even philosophy. In the upcoming years particular attention will be paid to history for these reasons.

Have the child read the text and the supplementary works for each culture. As the reading for one civilization is completed use the exercises at the end of the chapter either as reinforcement, or for a test revealing how well the material covered is remembered and grasped. Then have the child write a paper incorporating the material about each subject from the various sources.

This will encourage note taking skills, the ability to organize information from reference materials, and the application of proper word usage, punctuation, and spelling to written reports.

## GEOGRAPHY — MAP STUDY WITH AN HISTORICAL ATLAS (2)

Use the historical atlas in conjunction with your history studies and have your child draw maps for each civilization as he studies it. Keep the maps in a binder with the papers he writes in History and at the end of the year there will be an illustrated ancient history, which may be added to in subsequent years. Eventually your child will have a world history of his own production, an impressive achievement.

## LATIN — *Latin Grammar, Book I* BY DOUGLAS WILSON (3)

*Latin Grammar* builds on the vocabulary and paradigm knowledge presented in the previous book. The children continue to practice the paradigms and do simple translations. This is an excellent text, partly because it does not move too quickly. It allows the children to make the information habitual, not just store it in the short term memory.

## ART — *Draw Today* (8), ART BOOKS FROM THE LIBRARY, CRAFTS

I have not used *Draw Today,* though I anticipate doing so. I include it here as an alternative to the suggestions I have made for previous years, though those materials, *Drawing Textbook* for example, could certainly be used again.

*Draw Today,* a portrait drawing course, is appealing because it combines classical drawing techniques and easy to follow instructions. The distributors, Greenleaf Press, have used the program and they like it. It is guaranteed, so if you are not satisfied with your set, even after using it, you may return it for the entire purchase price!

The remainder of the year use good quality art books for art discussions, particularly discussions of portraits, using the knowledge you have gained from *Draw Today* and *Drawing Textbook.*

Also encourage crafts such as sewing (you could have a skirt making class) or quilting (make a small quilt) or wood working. Cooking is an artistic craft and a wonderful skill to have. Both boys and girls can profit by instruction in this area.

## MUSIC — BALLET MUSIC AND VIDEOS, GILBERT AND SULLIVAN MUSIC AND VIDEOS, OTHER FAVORITES

Children enjoy listening to familiar music in context. Ballets and operettas are more enjoyable when the music is known and the action of the story clear. I have included a few possibilities for this kind of music appreciation at the end of this section, as well as some of our own favorites to listen to.

## TENTATIVE SCHEDULE FOR SIXTH GRADE

| MON. | TUES. | WED. | THURS. | FRI. |
|---|---|---|---|---|
| MATH | MATH | MATH | MATH | MATH |
| ENGLISH | ENGLISH | ENGLISH | ENGLISH | LITERATURE |
| GEOGRAPHY | RELIGION | RELIGION | SCIENCE | MUSIC |
| RELIGION | ART | LATIN | RELIGION | |
| HISTORY | LATIN | HISTORY | LATIN | |

# Grade Six Resource Lists

## Religion Study Guide for Sixth Grade— Questions for St. Mark's Gospel

CHAPTER 1

   1. In the first 15 verses, does it seem that the teaching of John and Jesus is the same? In what way is it the same and in what way (if anything) is it different?

   2. Jesus says He has come to preach in verse 38. Where else in this chapter is there evidence that His teaching was more important to Him than His miracles?

CHAPTER 2

   1. Answer the question in verse 9 and give a reason for your answer.

   2. Answer the question in verse 7.

   3. Find three names or descriptive terms that Jesus uses for himself.

CHAPTER 3

   1. In verse 27, what does the strong man represent? his house?

   2. For what work did Jesus select the twelve? What powers did He give them? How would these powers help them in their work?

CHAPTER 4

   1. In verse 11, to whom do you think Our Lord refers with the words "those outside"? Notice that the parable and its explanation are both preserved in Holy Scripture for all to read.

CHAPTER 5

   1. Do you think the people in verses 14-17 were more afraid of Jesus than they had been of the unclean spirit? What might they be afraid of (verse 16)?

   2. What does St. Mark say about why Jesus felt the touch of the

woman in verses 27-30 as distinct from the general press of the crowd? Why did He ask the question He did?

3. After what earlier miracles were people charged to tell no one of it, as in Verse 43? (Look in chapters 1 and 3.)

CHAPTER 6

1. What was the message of the Twelve when Jesus sent them out two by two? Was it a new message or had it been previously announced by another?

2. In verse 34, Mark says Jesus began to teach the crowd, but He had come to that desert place for another reason. What was it?

CHAPTER 7

1. What does Our Lord mean in verse 15 by the things that enter a man from the outside? What would His listeners first think of as "things that enter from outside" when discussing the laws of cleanliness?

2. In verse 27, who are the "children"?

3. How is the healing in verses 28-30 like that in Ch. 5:28-34? How is it unlike?

4. How is the manner of healing in verses 31-36 different from that in Ch. 5:38-43? How is it alike?

CHAPTER 8

1. Can you tell when or where the bread is multiplied? (After___, but before___.)

2. Think of what leaven does to bread; what leaven is like before and after it is put in bread. Leaven is useful, indeed, necessary in making bread. It also smells good. In these ways it is unlike the Pharisees and Herod. How might it be like these dangers?

3. In verses 26 and 30, who is told not to speak, and what is he told not to speak about? Do you think that this silence is to be temporary or permanent? Why do you think so?

4. In verse 35, does "gospel" refer to "a certain book of Holy Scripture" or "this good news"? How can you tell?

CHAPTER 9

1. In the Transfiguration account, find another piece of evidence that Jesus' teaching was more important than His miracles.

2. Jesus again tells someone to not tell others, but now He also says when he can tell. Whom does He tell and when is the silence to end?

3. In the cure of the possessed boy, Our Lord asks for something from the father. Can you see things in the father's response that must have pleased Jesus?

4. The disciples could not cast out this unclean spirit. What other evidence is there that this was a particularly powerful or difficult spirit to cast out?

5. In verse 31, the disciples are said to be "afraid." What can this mean?

CHAPTER 10

1. Before it was the sick who sought to be touched by Jesus. Why do these people want Jesus to touch their children? Is touching a physical or spiritual act here?

2. Why are the ten angry at James and John? Explain how Jesus turns away their anger.

CHAPTER 11

1. Why did Our Lord throw out the money changers?

2. What happened to the fig tree that had no fruit? What might this be a sign of?

3. Our Lord says that we should forgive when we start to pray. What reason does He give?

CHAPTER 12

1. Whom did Jesus speak the parable of the vineyard about? (verse 12) Why?

2. What is Jesus' answer to those who wish to catch him in His words? (verse 13)

3. How did the Sadducees err in their question about who the

woman with the seven husbands would be married to in heaven?

4. In what way did the poor widow put in more money than all the others?

CHAPTER 13

1. Why will we be hated by all men? (verse 13)

2. What are the various things Our Lord warns us about in this chapter?

CHAPTER 14

1. Why was what the woman with the ointment did acceptable? Why did those who grumbled do so?

2. Who betrays Jesus, and what does he receive for this act? What does Our Lord say about him?

3. Who goes with Jesus to Gethsemani? What does He do there? What do they do?

4. Did Peter betray Christ? Is he like Judas in this? How does he differ from Judas?

5. What did Jesus say that the high priest objected to? How did those around Our Lord act once judgment was pronounced?

CHAPTER 15

1. Why had the chief priests delivered up Jesus? Does Pilate know this? Why does he have Jesus crucified?

2. Why does the Centurion who is present at the Crucifixion say, "Indeed this man was the Son of God"?

CHAPTER 16

1. Where is Peter singled out from the other disciples? Why do you think that might be?

2. Did those who heard Jesus was alive believe it? What did Jesus say to them when He appeared?

3. What did Jesus tell the disciples to do?

## LITERATURE LIST FOR SIXTH GRADE

Most of these are in print and they are all good. See *Honey for a Child's Heart* by Hunt for more titles.

| | |
|---|---|
| *Mrs. Frisby and the Rats of NIMH* | ROBERT C. O'BRIAN |
| *The Moffats* | ELEANOR ESTES |
| *Understood Betsy* | DOROTHY CANFIELD FISHER |
| *The Melendy Family* | ELIZABETH ENRIGHT |
| *The Wolves of Willoughby Chase* | JOAN AIKEN |
| *Black Hearts in Battersea* | JOAN AIKEN |
| *Nightbirds on Nantucket* | JOAN AIKEN |
| *Rebecca of Sunnybrook Farm* | KATE DOUGLAS WIGGIN |
| *All of a Kind Family* | SYDNEY TAYLOR |
| *Thimble Summer* | ELIZABETH ENRIGHT |
| *Miracles on Maple Hill* | VIRGINIA SORENSON |
| *Blue Willow* | DORIS GATES |
| *The Singing Tree* | KATE SEREDY |
| *The Good Master* | KATE SEREDY |
| *Snow Treasure* | MARIE McSWIGAN |
| *The Secret Cave* | CLAIRE HUCHET BISHOP |
| *Captains Courageous* | RUDYARD KIPLING |
| *The Island of the Blue Dolphins* | SCOTT O'DELL |
| *The Book of Valour* | FAITH AND FREEDOM 7 READING BOOK |
| *Daniel Boone* | JAMES DAUGHERTY |
| *The Railway Children* | E. NESBIT |
| *The House of Arden* | E. NESBIT |
| *The Phoenix and the Carpet* | E. NESBIT |
| *Five Children and It* | E. NESBIT |
| *The Treasure Seekers* | E. NESBIT |
| *The New Treasure Seekers* | E. NESBIT |
| *The Children Who Stayed Alone* | BONNIE WORLINE |
| *Brighty Of the Grand Canyon* | MARGUERITE HENRY |
| *My Side Of the Mountain* | JEAN GEORGE |
| *The Twenty-One Balloons* | WILLIAM PENE DUBOIS |
| *The Matchlock Gun* | W.D. EDWARDS |

| | | |
|---|---|---|
| *Born Free* | JOY ADAMSON | |
| *Big Red* | JIM KJELGAARD | |
| *Caddie Woodlawn* | CAROL RYRIE BRINK | |
| *The Door in the Wall* | MARGUERITE DE ANGELI | |
| *Swallows and Amazons* | ARTHUR RANSOME | |
| *Rip Van Winkle* | WASHINGTON IRVING | |
| *Smokey* | WILL JAMES | |

# HISTORY READING LIST FOR SIXTH GRADE— ANCIENT CIVILIZATIONS

Used as supplements to *The Old World and America* by Fr. Philip Furlong (Part I).

An "L" after the author's name indicates that the library or used book sources will be your best bet for securing this title, "IP" indicates that the book is currently in print, "*" indicates an especially enjoyable book. If a book belongs to an identifiable series I will indicate that by using one of the following abbreviations: VB — Vision Book (Catholic), AMB — American Background Book (Catholic), LKB — Landmark Book (Christian orientation), SB — Signature Book, NSB — North Star Book.

USBORNE BOOKS:
*World History Dates*
*Warriors and Seafarers*
*Book of Long Ago —*
   *Pharaohs and Pyramids*

| | | |
|---|---|---|
| *The 22 Letters* | CLIVE KING | L, * |
| *Pyramid* | DAVID MACAULAY | L, * |
| *The Amulet* | E. NESBIT | IP, * |
| *The Pharaohs of Ancient Egypt* | ELIZABETH PAYNE | IP, * LKB |
| *The World Of the Pharaohs* | HANS BAUMANN | L |
| *Piankhy, The Great* | E. HARPER JOHNSON | L |
| *Egyptian Adventures* | OLIVIA COOLIDGE | L, * |
| *The Book of History* | OLIVE BEAUPRE MILLER AND HARRY NEAL BAUM | L, * |
| *Mara, Daughter of the Nile* | ELOISE JARVIS MCGRAW | IP |

*The Golden Goblet*  Eloise Jarvis McGraw  IP
See Greenleaf Press for more titles (8)

## Poetry List for Sixth Grade

"The Charge of the
 Light Brigade"  Alfred Lord Tennyson
"Opportunity"  Edward Sill
"Father William"  Robert Southey
"The Lake Isle of
 Innisfree"  William Butler Yeats
"The Old Woman of
 the Roads"  Padraic Colum
"Be Strong"  Maltbie D. Babcock
"The Night Has a
 Thousand Eyes"  Francis W. Bourdillon
"The Violet"  Jane Taylor
"The Builders"  Henry Wadsworth Longfellow
"Jabberwocky"  Lewis Carroll
"The Children's Hour"  Henry Wadsworth Longfellow

## Music List for Sixth Grade

Tchaikovsky
 *The Nutcracker,*
  music and video
 *Sleeping Beauty,*
  music and video

Vaughn Williams
 *English Folksongs*
 *Dives and Lazarus*
 *Five Mystical Songs*

Copeland
 *American Folksongs*
 *Appalachian Spring*

Mozart
 *The Magic Flute*
 *The Clarinet Quintet*

Gilbert and Sullivan
 *The Pirates of Penzance,*
  music and video
 *The Mikado,*
  music and video

# NOTES

# The
# Dialectical
# Stage

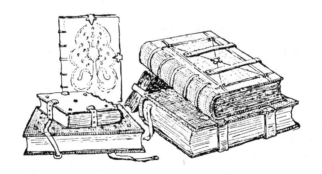

# The Dialectical Stage

THE NEXT STAGE OF THE TRIVIUM begins sometime around seventh grade. There is a certain overlap of levels, and one continues to gather materials for the dialectic stage, even when it has begun. Nevertheless, there is a change in emphasis from the grammar of subjects, employing observation and memory, to the dialectic of subjects, which uses the discursive reason.

This difference is seen in the importance *analysis* has in the curriculum. In language grammar the children will continue to diagram sentences, which is an analytic exercise. They will also learn about the nature of language by using a text that compares Latin and English grammar.

In history and religion they will begin to concentrate on seeing the reasons for actions and positions. First they must see clearly what is being said, and then why. There will be reasonable arguments given for opposing positions and then a resolution proposed based on ethical and dogmatic principles. This will be done both in writing and in conversation.

Literature will concern itself with the same method. Careful reading of a text and the presentation of the position will be the focus of the courses. Because men learn by imitation, the careful study of others' arguments will provide examples of what the student will learn to do. The study of poetry will center on dramatic performances, particularly plays, wherein an argument is stated in dramatic form.

Mathematics moves to the more advanced forms, algebra and geometry. In these studies the nature of the subject matter, where the mind moves from premise to premise, is seen clearly. In my curriculum I try not to make this particular change abruptly, or too soon. I have found a slower, more thorough, approach is better.

Science and geography provide other material for the practice of the method of dialectic. Geography is often incorporated in historical discussions, contributing to the understanding of why someone acted as he did.

Religion is moving toward dogmatic theology, with the kind of treatment of Scripture that was begun last year as a beginning step.

All of these subjects are intended to provide an opportunity for analysis, for learning how to understand and produce an argument. It is a way of studying Logic, not as one will study it in Aristotle's *Prior and Posterior Analytics,* but in a way that prepares the student for that study.

In "The Lost Tools of Learning" Miss Sayers says of this stage, "All events are food for such an appetite. An umpire's decision; the degree to which one may transgress the spirit of a regulation without being trapped by the letter: on such questions as these, children are born casuists, and their natural propensity only needs to be developed and trained — and, especially, be brought into intelligible relationship with events in the grown-up world."

# Seventh Grade Curriculum

**Sources for items followed by a number in parentheses may be found at the back of the book under the suppliers list.**

RELIGION — LIVES OF THE SAINTS (4), NEW TESTAMENT *(Acts)*, *The Story of the Church* BY FR. GEORGE JOHNSON, FR. JEROME HANNAN AND SR. M. DOMINICA (14)

In the first six weeks, read various lives of the saints. Choose a saint each week from the list provided at the end of this section. Read about the saint and prepare an oral report. The saints on the list are contemporaneous with the period being studied in History in the latter part of the year.

The next 18 weeks will be devoted to a detailed study of the *Acts of the Apostles*. Read and discuss the text every week. I have included a list of discussion questions at the end of this section. *The Bronze Bow* by Elizabeth George Speare, and *The Glorious Folly* by Louis De Wohl will help give a sense of the period in which the *Acts* takes place.

During the last twelve weeks study early Church history from the beginning of the Church through 300 A.D. This will bring secular history and Church history together as one whole.

MATHEMATICS — *Math 87* (SAXON) (3)

This text is a bridge between basic arithmetic and algebra. Have the child do a lesson in the text everyday and monitor his progress by use of the tests that come with the homeschool packet. The student will develop a certain facility in computation and understanding of principles and proofs.

GRAMMAR AND COMPOSITION — *Voyages in English 7* (12), PAPERS IN HISTORY, *Learning Language Arts Through Literature* (GRAY BOOK) (3)

As I have said before, grammar is important both as a tool for understanding language itself, and for mastering other languages. It is also important because this is an area that a seventh grader can comprehend. It is proportioned to the capacity of the student in a way that most subjects are not at this age. A child must study and have a disciplined mind in order to accomplish this, but it can be done. Achieving this at this time of life, in an area where it can truly be done, shows the child what intellectual mastery is, and what a satisfaction it is.

The writing instructions in the Gray Book seem to be more effective for most children than the writing portions of *Voyages in English*. Follow the order of the text, doing one lesson per week. In each lesson there will be two days of dictation, a certain number of opportunities for practice in composition and punctuation, and practice in analytic grammar.

REFERENCE SKILLS — *Information Please!* BY PAT WESOLOWSKI (3) OR A WORKBOOK FROM YOUR LOCAL EDUCATIONAL SUPPLY STORE.

*Information Please!* is a practical, hands-on supplement that teaches the proper use of reference materials by giving children an opportunity to use them. It provides worksheets of items the student needs to look up information about. Figuring out where to find the necessary information is the key to success.

Your local educational supply store may also have a workbook that would help your child sort out what reference source to use when. We have found this to be one area where a workbook is actually helpful.

SPELLING AND VOCABULARY — *Wordly Wise 4* (22)

Follow the internal order of the text, doing one lesson each week. Use the vocabulary words for a spelling list, and give tests once a week. This text has a useful vocabulary and teaches about word origins and relationships, which fits with the study of the nature of language.

LITERATURE — (CORRELATED WITH HISTORY) *Books Children Love* BY ELIZABETH WILSON (3), GREENLEAF PRESS BOOKS (8), *In Review* (9), *Catholic Authors: 4-Sight Edition* BY THE BROTHERS OF MARY (10), *Honey for a Child's Heart* BY GLADYS HUNT (3) *Let the Authors Speak* BY CAROLYN HATCHER (15)

In this year literature and history are virtually identical. The history list provides ample reading material, and other texts can be found in the books I mention above. The books studied will help the student understand the beginnings of western civilization. This understanding is important for political prudence and right judgment. History is interesting in itself, but it also provides vicarious experience about events and people.

POETRY — SHAKESPEARE (1), *Tales from Shakespeare* BY CHARLES AND MARY LAMB (1), *Shake Hands with Shakespeare* BY ALBERT CULLUM (7)

Memorizing beautiful and evocative passages from Shakespeare will improve the child's knowledge of rhetorical patterns, encourage imitation and give the children familiarity with one of the greatest English authors. Use *Shake Hands with Shakespeare* as a guide, or simply do some editing of Shakespeare yourself, and whole plays or portions of plays may be attempted. The children enjoy dramatization and using beautiful words. These activities will give them an opportunity to do so, and lead them to a lifetime love of Shakespeare.

One way to introduce Shakespeare is to pick a selection from the list at the end of this section. Have the child read the play in *Tales from Shakespeare,* then memorize the passages chosen, and then read the play in Shakespeare. If the child is then able to see the play performed he will have a good basis for real enjoyment of the production.

SCIENCE — *Concepts and Challenges in Science* (B) BY ALAN WINKLER, LEONARD BERNSTEIN, MARTIN SCHACHTER AND STANLEY WOLFE (PUBLISHED BY GLOBE) (25), FABRE BOOKS (7,1)

Four times a week read the text and do the exercises in each chapter. Unit tests will provide a check of comprehension. This text, like the previous volume, concentrates on a basic understanding of biology and physics, chemistry and earth science. There is not a great deal of detail, but there are clear explanations of the principles.

Most of the Fabre books are out of print. I will mention some titles to look for because they are wonderful examples of natural history, the kind of thing that will lead to love for and understanding of nature. They fit very well with this stage of the Trivium because they explore why the animals act the way they do. *Our Humble Helpers, The Life of the Spider,* and *The Insect World of J. Henri Fabre* are some of Fabre's works. Of these only the last is currently in print.

HISTORY — BOOKS ABOUT ANCIENT GREECE AND ROME (8), *The Old World and America* BY FR. PHILIP FURLONG (14) *Let the Authors Speak* BY CAROLYN HATCHER (15)

As I mentioned before, *The Old World and America* is an excellent text. This is the text I recommend using for sixth, seventh, and eighth grades because it is interesting, has good exercises and a Catholic perspective.

It is worthwhile to have the student answer the questions of the exercises completely, citing the portion of the text where the answer was found. This gives the child a chance to practice locating material in a text, which leads to attentive reading. Make sure that the answers are logical, and that the reasons given for the answers make sense.

This course concentrates on the beginning of western civilization, the personalities and events in the Greek and Roman civilizations. A list of supplementary readings is included at the end of this section. I have also included a list of significant dates the student may memorize. The child who enjoys writing narrative summaries may continue his "book of history."

Though I have included many readings on my list, not all are equally important. I have starred those that are particularly good and recommend that you start with those and read the rest as time permits. There are other texts about the same time period which can be found in *Let the Authors Speak.*

GEOGRAPHY — *Mapping the World by Heart* BY DAVID SMITH (18) *or* DRAWING MAPS OF THE ANCIENT WORLD TO GO WITH THE HISTORY TEXT.

*Mapping the World by Heart* is a relatively new program that looks like fun. I have not used it, but I have done something like it on my own. The text comes with a video that illustrates the program, and it is written by a teacher who has been using it for 15 years. The aim of the program is to be able to make detailed world maps from memory. This is achieved in small units with daily repetition.

If this is done successfully, "the students have accomplished [a] mastery of a body of knowledge which they considered impossible nine months earlier. They have acquired a foundation on which to place any geographical references they come to in their reading and learning, and on which to build as they progress through school and beyond."

LATIN — *Basic Language Principles Through Latin Background* BY RUTH M. WILSON (21)

This is an outstanding book. It solidifies the child's grasp of English grammar and provides an excellent beginning in Latin. It moves slowly and carefully, with plenty of opportunity for practice. Use this and you will never forget the first and second declensions and the first conjugation. And most children really like it — not because of a flamboyant format (it doesn't have that) but because of intellectual satisfaction.

There are fifty lessons, so you need to start out with more than one lesson a week. That way when you get to the more challenging lessons you will be able to do one lesson each week and still finish the text in a year.

The only drawback to this text is that you have to do the exercises too. There is no answer key. If you are a Latin whiz that is not a problem, but most of us aren't, and so we have to work it out step by step. I am working on a key for this text.

ART — *Art Smart!* BY SUSAN RODRIGUEZ (17) *or* ANY OF THE PREVIOUS YEARS' SUGGESTIONS

*Art Smart!* features a hands on approach to art appreciation. It comes with 40 slides of works of art and a lesson plan to go with each one. The lessons include information about the artist and directions for producing a similar work. (Similar can be said in many ways!) If you don't want to clutter your house with art media this is not for you, but if you like that kind of thing it is a great program.

**MUSIC — *Music Smart!* BY GWEN HOTCHKISS (17)**

*Music Smart!* comes with three tapes and many lesson plans. The lesson plans are very complete and you can use as much or as little of the material as you want. The information is interesting and well presented. And the text includes the music scores for the pieces on the tapes! This is where all the previous music theory you have done pays off. It is fun to follow the music on the score.

## TENTATIVE SCHEDULE FOR SEVENTH GRADE

| Mon. | Tues. | Wed. | Thurs. | Fri. |
|---|---|---|---|---|
| MATH | MATH | MATH | MATH | MATH |
| ENGLISH | ENGLISH | ENGLISH | ENGLISH | LITERATURE |
| SCIENCE | SCIENCE | SCIENCE | SCIENCE | SCIENCE |
| GEOGRAPHY | MUSIC | RELIGION | ART | |
| RELIGION | RELIGION | HISTORY | RELIGION | |
| HISTORY | HISTORY | LATIN | HISTORY | |
| LATIN | LATIN | | LATIN | |

# Grade Seven Resource Lists

## Religion Study Guide for Seventh Grade— Questions for the Acts of the Apostles

### Chapter 1

1. What is the full title of Acts?
2. The book begins right after an important event, or series of events. What is it? or What are they?
3. Jesus gave the Apostles a final instruction. What did He say? And what happened next?
4. What city do the Apostles go to after the Ascension?
5. How was Matthias chosen to be an Apostle? Whose place did he take?
6. Why does Peter conduct the election?

### Chapter 2

1. Which came first, Pentecost or the Ascension?
2. Describe the events of the coming of the Holy Spirit. They were together in one place and ... (1, 2, 3, 4)
3. People heard about this amazing event and gathered together. What surprised them?
4. Who first said, "And it shall come to pass in the last days (saith the Lord), I will pour out of my Spirit upon all flesh ..."? What was he talking about?
5. Who first said, "You (God) wilt not leave my soul in hell, nor suffer thy Holy One to see corruption, ..."?
6. To whom did he refer?
7. Why did Peter tell them that Joel and David were talking about Christ?
8. What did Peter tell the Jews they should do?
9. How many were converted that day?
10. What signs of charity and divine favor attended the first Christian community?

CHAPTER 3

1. Speaking in tongues preceded Peter's great sermon in Ch.2. Here, another miracle precedes Peter's second great sermon. What is it?

2. How does Peter heal a man? What does he say about how he was healed?

3. In this sermon what does Peter exhort the people to do?

CHAPTER 4

1. How many people had now come to believe in Our Lord?

2. Who apprehends Peter and John? What do you think Peter says that makes them angry?

3. What does the council tell the Apostles to do? Did Peter and John agree to this?

4. When Peter and John went back to their own company what happened?

CHAPTER 5

1. What was the sin of Ananias and Sapphira?

2. Why were the Apostles apprehended the second time?

3. Did they stay in prison?

4. Why has Peter disobeyed the order of the council not to preach the Name of Jesus?

5. Who urged moderation on the council and what was he?

6. What punishment did the Apostles receive?

CHAPTER 6

1. For what service were Stephen and six others selected?

2. With what ceremony were they selected?

3. In what ways was Stephen outstanding in the Christian community?

4. Of what did the false witnesses accuse him?

5. What indicates that Stephen's speech in response was inspired by the Holy Spirit?

CHAPTER 7

1. Stephen tells the council, "As your fathers did, so do you." What did their fathers do?
2. And what did the Jewish leaders of his day do?
3. What is Stephen's last act?
4. Why do you think the Roman government is not involved in this first persecution of the Church?

CHAPTER 8

1. What happened immediately after the martyrdom of Stephen?
2. Who preached the good news of Christ to the Samaritans?
3. How did they receive it?
4. What did Peter and John add to the baptisms in Samaria?
5. What was Simon's sin?
6. Why did Philip leave Samaria?
7. What was God's plan for him on the road to Gaza?

CHAPTER 9

1. Saul had a purpose in going to Damascus. What was it?
2. The Lord had a purpose for Saul. What does He tell Ananias that Saul has been chosen to do?
3. What did Saul do after he regained his sight?
4. Where did Saul begin to preach?
5. Why did he leave? How?
6. Why were the disciples afraid of Saul in Jerusalem?
7. What miracle does Peter work at Lydda?
8. Who is Tabitha?
9. What does Peter do for her?

CHAPTER 10

1. What was Cornelius' job?
2. In what two acts did he show his piety?
3. What did the voice tell Peter after his vision of the animals?

4. Peter interprets this to mean that he can do something further (not connected with eating) that the Jews have not been permitted to do. What?

5. What did those who came with Peter see which showed them that the Holy Spirit had indeed come upon the gentiles there?

6. What does "those of the circumcision" mean?

CHAPTER 11

1. What saying of Jesus does Peter recall which he can now understand as supporting his baptism of gentiles?

2. Where next was the gospel preached to non-Jews? Who preached there?

3. What prophecy was made there?

CHAPTER 12

1. How did Herod persecute the church at this time?

2. What did the angel who came to the prison do for Peter?

3. What did he tell Peter to do himself?

4. Why was Herod struck dead?

CHAPTER 13

1. What were the Christians in the church at Antioch doing when the Holy Spirit spoke, telling them to set apart Paul and Barnabas?

2. What did Saul do to the sorcerer attached to the pro-consul on Cyprus?

3. What effect did this have on the pro-consul?

4. In both Cyprus and Pisidia Antioch, where is the first place Saul and Barnabas go to preach?

5. In Paul's speech at Pisidia Antioch, how does he say the inhabitants of Jerusalem fulfilled the prophecies?

6. How does Paul say God has fulfilled the promise made to their fathers?

7. What does Paul say he will do when the Jews reject the word he preached?

CHAPTER 14

1. What did the people in Lystra think of Paul and Barnabas when Paul cured the man lame from his birth?

2. In each of the cities in this chapter, why do they have to leave?

CHAPTER 15

1. What question did Paul and Barnabas go to Jerusalem to discuss?

2. Who said, "Why then do you now try to test God by putting on the neck of the disciples a yoke which neither our fathers nor we have been able to bear?"

3. Which of the following restrictions did the council decide were still necessary?

   a. circumcision            e. abstaining from things offered to idols

   b. abstaining from blood   f. ritual hand washing

   c. not marrying foreigners g. abstaining from anything strangled

   d. abstaining from pork    h. avoiding immorality

CHAPTER 16

1. Why did Paul circumcise Timothy?

2. In what two ways did the churches improve?

3. How did Paul decide what cities to travel to?

4. Who insisted that Paul stay in her house in Macedonia?

5. Why did the masters of the possessed girl bring Paul and Silas before the magistrates?

6. What did they accuse Paul and Silas of?

7. How were they freed from their imprisonment?

8. Why did the guard want to kill himself?

9. What did Paul want to be done before he would leave the prison?

CHAPTER 17

1. Paul and his companions came to Thessalonica. What did they do there? And for how long?

2. What happened and why?

3. Next Paul went to Berea. How did the Jews there receive him?

4. What happened at Berea? Where did Paul go next?

5. Paul preaches to the Athenians. What idea does he use to begin telling them about Jesus? Why does he use this instead of the Law and the Prophets of the Old Testament?

CHAPTER 18

1. Was Paul successful with the Jews at Corinth?

2. What did Jesus tell Paul he should do?

3. Why did the Jews bring Paul before Gallio? What did Gallio say?

4. What did Apollo do for the Church?

CHAPTER 19

1. Had the members of the Church in Ephesus been baptized?

2. Paul found that, after three months, certain of those in the synagogue were hardened, speaking evil of the way of the Lord. What did he do?

3. Could anyone cure using the way of the Lord?

4. Why was the man Demetrius upset about the way of the Lord? What did he do?

5. How does the town clerk quiet the tumult?

CHAPTER 20

1. Can you see, in verse 4, a sign of the catholicity of the Catholic Church?

2. What miracle did Paul do at Troas?

3. What are the important points of Paul's discourse?

CHAPTER 21

1. Does Paul know what awaits him at Jerusalem?

2. What advice do those in Jerusalem give him?

3. Did this appease those who were angry with Paul?

4. What did those men intend to do to Paul? Why didn't they do it?

CHAPTER 22

1. Paul speaks to the multitude and they listen until what point? Why did this make them so angry?

2. The centurion is going to scourge and torture Paul. Why doesn't he do it?

CHAPTER 23

1. What device does Paul use to deflect interest from himself?
2. How does Paul escape from the plot of the Jews?
3. Where is Paul sent?
4. Does the governor hear Paul's case immediately?

CHAPTER 24

1. Who comes to accuse Paul? Of what do they accuse him?
2. What is his defense?
3. What does Felix do?
4. Why do you think Felix was terrified by the things Paul preached?

CHAPTER 25

1. Felix asks Paul if he will go to Jerusalem to be judged. Paul objects. What are his grounds?
2. What does Paul do now?
3. Who comes and wishes to hear Paul?

CHAPTER 26

1. What kind of Jew had Paul been?
2. What did King Agrippa think of Paul's account?

CHAPTER 27

1. Did Paul go alone to Rome?
2. Does Paul think it advisable to sail from Crete? Is he right? How does he know?
3. How many people were in the ship? How many were saved?

CHAPTER 28

1. Why did the Melitians think Paul was a god?
2. Paul comes to Rome and calls together the chief of the Jews. He explains why he is there. He tells them also of Jesus. Do they believe?
3. What does Paul say of them?

# SAINT LIST FOR SEVENTH GRADE

| | |
|---|---|
| ST. AGNES | ST. JOHN CHRYSOSTOM |
| ST. LUCY | ST. AMBROSE |
| ST. LAWRENCE | ST. JEROME |
| ST. CYPRIAN OF CARTHAGE | ST. AUGUSTINE |
| ST. JUSTIN | ST. LEO THE GREAT |
| ST. IRENEUS | (ORIGEN, TERTULLIAN) |
| ST. ATHANASIUS | |

# POETRY LIST FOR SEVENTH GRADE— SHAKESPEARE

THE TEMPEST       ACT V, I, 22-71

"This rough magic I here abjure ..."

HAMLET       ACT I, III, 22-116

"This above all: to thine own self be true,"

JULIUS CAESAR       ACT III, II, 37-71

"Friends, Romans, countrymen ..."

HENRY V       ACT IV, III, 1-81

"This day is called the feast of Crispian ..."

HENRY V       ACT IV, I, 224-281

"Upon the king! let us our lives, our souls, Our debts, our careful wives, Our children and our sins lay on the king!"

# HISTORY DATES LIST FOR SEVENTH GRADE

| | | |
|---|---:|---|
| (B.C.) | c. 1200 | TROJAN WAR |
| | c. 1050 | KING DAVID |
| | c. 753 | ROMULUS AND REMUS FOUND ROME. |
| | c. 630 | LYCURGUS GIVES LAWS TO SPARTA. |
| | 586 | NEBUCHADNEZZER'S ARMY SACKS JERUSALEM. |
| | 515 | TEMPLE IS REDEDICATED. |
| | 509 | ROMAN REPUBLIC BEGINS WITH EXPULSION OF TARQUIN KINGS. |
| | 490 | DARIUS IS DEFEATED AT THE BATTLE OF MARATHON. |

| | |
|---|---|
| 479 | SPARTAN DEFENSE OF THERMOPYLAE; XERXES IS DEFEATED AT SALAMIS (NAVAL) AND PLATAEA (LAND). |
| 438 | THE PARTHENON IS COMPLETED UNDER PERICLES' LEADERSHIP. |
| 404 | PELEPONNESIAN WAR ENDS WITH SPARTA DEFEATING ATHENS. |
| 401 | XENOPHON'S "ANABASIS"—"MARCH OF THE 10,000" |
| 399 | EXECUTION OF SOCRATES |
| 390 | GAULS SACK ROME. |
| 336 | ALEXANDER BECOMES KING OF MACEDONIA. |
| C. 300 | EUCLID'S GEOMETRY IS WRITTEN. |
| 202 | SCIPIO DEFEATS HANNIBAL. |
| 160 | RISE OF THE MACCHABEES |
| 133 | TIBERIUS GRACCHUS IS KILLED IN SENATE. |
| 60 | JERUSALEM IS CAPTURED BY POMPEY. |
| 44 | JULIUS CAESAR BECOMES DICTATOR OF ROME. |
| 31 | OCTAVIUS DEFEATS ANTONY AND CLEOPATRA AT ACTIUM. |
| 27 | AUGUSTUS CAESAR (FORMERLY OCTAVIUS) BECOMES FIRST CITIZEN. |

| (A.D.) | | |
|---|---|---|
| | 29 | CRUCIFIXION OF OUR LORD (REFORMED CALENDAR) |
| | 123 | HADRIAN'S WALL IS COMPLETED IN BRITAIN. |
| | 313 | CONSTANTINE ISSUES EDICT OF MILAN. |
| | 395 | ROMAN EMPIRE IS DIVIDED. |
| | 430 | AUGUSTINE, BISHOP OF HIPPO, DIES. |
| | 476 | END OF THE ROMAN EMPIRE IN THE WEST. |

## HISTORY READING LIST FOR SEVENTH GRADE— ANCIENT GREEK HISTORY

Used as supplements to *The Old World and America* by Fr. Philip Furlong (Part II) (pp. 25-61 in the 1984 edition published by TAN Books)

An "L" after the author's name indicates that the library or used book sources will be your best bet for securing this title, "IP" indicates that the book is currently in print, "*" indicates an especially enjoyable book. If a book belongs to an identifiable series I will indicate that by using one of the following abbreviations. VB — Vision Book (Catholic), AMB — American Background Book (Catholic), LKB — Landmark Book (Christian orientation), SB — Signature Book, NSB — North Star Book

| | | |
|---|---|---|
| *Greek Myths* | INGRI AND EDGAR D'AULAIRE | IP, * |
| *The Greek Army* | PETER CONNOLLY | IP |
| *Empires and Barbarians* | (USBORNE) | IP |
| *Lives from Plutarch: The Modern American Edition of Twelve* | EDITED BY JOHN McFARLAND | L, * |
| *Children's Homer* | PADRAIC COLUM | IP, * |
| *The Histories* | HERODOTUS (TRANSLATED BY AUBREY DE SELINCOURT PENGUIN BOOKS.) READ THE FOLLOWING PARTS: BK. VI, PP. 384-404 (MARATHON) BK. VII, PP. 413-584 (READ PAGES 413-438, 443, 447-449, 453-454, 457, 459-464, 475-498 IF PRESSED FOR TIME) (THERMOPYLAE) (PP. 499-539, 544, 547-550) (SALAMIS) (PP. 551-584) (PLATAEA) | IP, * |
| *Temple on a Hill* | ANN ROCKWELL | L, * |
| *Men of Athens* | OLIVIA COOLIDGE | L, * |
| *Theras and His Town* | CAROLINE SNEDEKER | L, * |
| *The White Isle* | CAROLINE SNEDEKER | L |
| *The Spartan* | CAROLINE SNEDEKER | L |
| *The Exploits of Xenophon* | GEOFFREY HOUSEHOLD | IP, * |
| *The Adventures of Odysseus* | ANDREW LANG | L |
| *The Trojan War* | OLIVIA COOLIDGE | IP, * |
| *Golden Days of Greece* | OLIVIA COOLIDGE | IP, * |

| | | |
|---|---|---|
| *Greek Myths* | OLIVIA COOLIDGE | IP |
| *A Wonder Book* | NATHANIEL HAWTHORNE | IP,* |
| *The Tale of Troy* | ROGER LANCELYN GREEN | IP,* |
| *The Golden Fleece* | PADRAIC COLUM | IP,* |
| *Tales of the Greek Heroes* | ROGER LANCELYN GREEN | IP,* |
| *Dolphin Rider* | BERNARD EVSLIN | L |
| *The Golden God* | DORIS GATES | IP |
| *The Greek Gods* | BERNARD EVSLIN, DOROTHY EVSLIN AND NED HOOPES | IP |
| *Heroes and Monsters of Greek Myth* | BERNARD EVSLIN, DOROTHY EVSLIN AND NED HOOPES | IP |
| *The Story of the Greeks* | H.A. GUERBER | L |
| *Children of the Dawn* | ELSIE FINNIMORE BUCKLEY | L,* |
| *The Heroes* | CHARLES KINGSLEY | L |
| *The Adventures of Ulysses* | GERALD GOTTLIEB | IP, LKB |
| *Fifteen Decisive Battles of the World* | EDWARD CREASY (MARATHON) | IP,* |
| *The Walls of Windy Troy* | MARJORIE BRAYMEN | L |
| *How We Learned the Earth was Round* | PATRICIA LAUBER | IP |
| *Black Ships Before Troy* | ROSEMARY SUTCLIFF | IP,* |
| *Greek and Roman Plays* | ALBERT CULLUM | IP,* |

## ANCIENT ROMAN HISTORY

Used as a supplement to *The Old World and America* by Fr. Philip Furlong (Chapters III–IV) (pp. 63–118 in the 1984 edition published by TAN Books)

| | | |
|---|---|---|
| *City* | DAVID MACAULAY | IP,* |
| "HORATIUS" FROM *The Lays of Ancient Rome* | THOMAS LORD MACAULAY | L,* |

| | | |
|---|---|---|
| *The Roman Army* | PETER CONNOLLY | L |
| *Empires and Barbarians* | (USBORNE) | IP |
| *Eagle of the Ninth* | ROSEMARY SUTCLIFF | IP, * |
| *The Silver Branch* | ROSEMARY SUTCLIFF | IP, * |
| *The Lantern Bearers* | ROSEMARY SUTCLIFF | IP, * |
| *A Triumph for Flavius* | CAROLINE SNEDEKER | L, * |
| *Lives from Plutarch:* | | |
| *The Modern American* | | |
| *Edition of Twelve* | EDITED BY JOHN | |
| | McFARLAND | L, * |
| *The Truce of the Games* | ROSEMARY SUTCLIFF | L |
| *Roman People* | OLIVIA COOLIDGE | L, * |
| *Caesar's Gallic Wars* | OLIVIA COOLIDGE | IP, * |
| *Lives of Famous Romans* | OLIVIA COOLIDGE | IP, * |
| *The Aeneid for Boys and Girls* | A.J. CHURCH | L, * |
| *Men of Rome* | OLIVIA COOLIDGE | L, * |
| *Julius Caesar* | JOHN GUNTHER | L, LKB |
| *St. Helena and the True Cross* | LOUIS DE WOHL | L, * VB |
| *Blood Feud* | ROSEMARY SUTCLIFF | L |
| *Christ the King, Lord* | | |
| *of History* (CHAPTER 6) | ANN CARROLL | IP, * |
| *Famous Battles by Land* | | |
| *and Sea* (CHAPTER 3) | EDITED BY THOMAS | |
| | BAILEY ALDRICH | L |
| *Living in Roman Times* | JANE CHISOLM | L |
| *Roman Engineers* | L.A. AND J.A. HAMEY | IP, * |
| *The Roman Army* | JOHN WILKES | IP |
| *The Young Carthaginian* | G.A. HENTY | L |
| *Life in Ancient Rome* | PIERRE MIQUEL | L |
| *The Romans and Their Empire* | TREVOR CAIRNS | IP |
| *Augustus Caesar* | MONROE STEARNS | IP, * |
| *Julius Caesar* | MANUEL KOMRUFF | L |
| *Legions of the Eagle* | HENRY TREECE | L, * |
| *Rome and Romans* | (USBORNE) | IP, * |
| *Ancient Rome* | SIMON JAMES | |
| | (EYE WITNESS BOOKS) | IP |
| *Two Thousand Years Ago* | A.J. CHURCH | L, * |

# Eighth Grade Curriculum

**Sources for items followed by a number in parentheses may be found at the back of the book under the suppliers list.**

RELIGION — *Faith and Life* 8TH GRADE TEXT *(Our Life in the Church)* WITH ACTIVITY BOOK (4), *Baltimore Catechism No. 2* (4), *The Case for Christianity* BY C.S. LEWIS (1)

The Faith and Life Catechism studies the doctrine of the Church on the sacraments in general and on Confirmation in particular. I recommend reading it with the corresponding chapters in the *Baltimore Catechism No. 2,* both because the questions and answers in the *Baltimore Catechism* are more succinct and because its treatment of the subjects is more formal. The statement of the doctrine is clearer in the *Baltimore Catechism.* In this way the two texts work well together; the Faith and Life text fleshes out or explains what is in the *Baltimore Catechism.* An even more thorough explanation of the doctrine is contained in *The Baltimore Catechism Explained* by Fr. Thomas L. Kincaid (14).

The Catechisms can be covered in the first part of the year and the second part given to a study of *The Case for Christianity.* I have included a study guide at the end of this section that will help the student see the argument in the text. This is a work that repays close attention on the part of the student. It is not too difficult for the eighth grader and he will enjoy seeing the argument Lewis gives for the Christian Faith.

MATHEMATICS — ALGEBRA ½ (SAXON) (3)

Algebra is a discipline that fits well with this stage of the Trivium. It employs argument, i.e. rational movement from one premise to the next, in a way that the student can follow fairly easily. This text is a good introduction to algebra and will prepare the student for the next level. As in all the other Saxon books there is a constant review of material so that a concept never has a chance to be forgotten.

GRAMMAR AND COMPOSITION — *Voyages in English 8* (12), PAPERS IN HISTORY, *Learning Language Arts Through Literature* (GOLD BOOK) (3)

Both grammar and writing exercises should be done regularly. When the student is working on a paper in History the writing text may be laid aside. Look at it at the beginning of the year and choose the exercises that seem best to you, then concentrate on those and forget the rest. Whatever the source of the student's writing, work diligently on re-writing. Have the child pay attention to reasoned positions. Does what he says follow from the opening premise? Does he actually answer the question? If he writes a narrative account, a re-telling of what happened, is it chronological? Do the paragraphs hold together, with one central idea for each? The student at this stage is capable of really thinking about these kinds of questions and revising his papers in the light of such considerations.

This is the last year that grammar will be studied intensively, so it should be a year of review and concentration on trouble spots. The most important, because most fundamental, thing the student should be able to do is break down a sentence into its parts. What is the simple subject, simple predicate, and object? That is the first step in analysis.

SPELLING AND VOCABULARY — *Wordly Wise 5* (21)

This text is the next in the series we used last year and should be used the same way. Follow the internal order of the text, doing one lesson each week. Use the vocabulary words for a spelling list, and give tests once a week. This text has a useful vocabulary and teaches word origins and relationships, which fits with the study of the nature of language.

LITERATURE — (CORRELATED WITH HISTORY) *Books Children Love* BY ELIZABETH WILSON (3), GREENLEAF PRESS BOOKS (8), *In Review* (9), ALSO *Catholic Authors: 4-sight Edition* AND *Catholic Authors: Crown Edition* BOTH BY THE BROTHERS OF MARY (10), *Honey for a Child's Heart* BY GLADYS HUNT (3), AND *Let the Authors Speak* BY CAROLYN HATCHER (15)

Though there will be numerous history readings this year I also include a literature list and mention other sources for lists. The child is able to read significantly more difficult material by this age and should be encouraged to do so. It would be best if the parent also reads the book and discusses it with the child. However, even if you are not able to read the book you should discuss it with your child. Have him tell you the story, and what ethical implications it has. Have your child characterize the people in the story. Discuss the author's point of view and whether it is also your point of view. This is the best way for your child to develop the critical skills he needs to read well.

The books that you choose to read and discuss with your child should not be the only books he reads. Each child should also be reading for the sheer enjoyment of it. Pick some of the books on the literature list for your discussions this year, but have the others in an accessible place and make time each day for reading. This is not wasted time, but an important formative activity. The book list I have included has many of my own favorites on it, but there are an abundance of other good books you might choose.

## POETRY — SHAKESPEARE (1), SEE LIST

Memorizing some of the sonnets and other passages from Shakespeare will continue to improve the child's knowledge of rhetorical patterns and encourage imitation.

I have included some other suggestions as well in the list at the end of this section.

## SCIENCE — *Concepts and Challenges in Science* (C) BY ALAN WINKLER, LEONARD BERNSTEIN, MARTIN SCHACHTER AND STANLEY WOLFE (PUBLISHED BY GLOBE) (25)

Four times a week read the text and do the exercises in each chapter. Unit tests provide a check of comprehension. This text, like the previous volumes, concentrates on a fundamental understanding of biology and physics, chemistry and earth science. There is not a great deal of detail, but there are clear explanations of the principles.

## HISTORY — BOOKS ABOUT MEDIEVAL TIMES (8), *The Old World and America* BY FR. PHILIP FURLONG (14) *Christ the King, Lord of History* BY ANNE CARROLL (20), *Let the Authors Speak* BY CAROLYN HATCHER (15)

As I mentioned before, *The Old World and America* is an excellent text. This is the text I recommend using for sixth, seventh, and eighth grades because it is interesting, has good exercises and a Catholic perspective. *Christ the King, Lord of History* is useful as an additional resource. It has an intensely Catholic perspective and information that is hard to find elsewhere.

It is worthwhile to have the student answer the questions of the exercises in *The Old World and America* completely, citing the portion of the text where the answer was found. This gives the child a chance to practice locating material in a text, which leads to attentive reading. Make sure that the answers are logical, and that the reasons given for the answers make sense.

This course concentrates on the Middle Ages, the personalities and events in medieval times. A list of supplementary readings is included at the end of this section, and other texts about the same time period can be found in *Let the Authors Speak.* I have also included a list of significant dates the student may memorize. The child who enjoys writing narrative summaries may continue his "book of history."

GEOGRAPHY — *Mapping the World by Heart* BY DAVID SMITH (18) OR DRAWING MAPS OF THE ANCIENT WORLD TO GO WITH THE HISTORY TEXT, *Explore Europe* (2), GEOGRAPHY LIST.

*Mapping the World by Heart* is the same program I recommended for last year. It may be used again to achieve mastery of this class. Pay special attention to the European maps because that will help with an understanding of the history program.

The game *Explore Europe* is fun and encourages a familiarity with European cities.

I have included a geography list to memorize at the end of this section. It includes European capitals, countries and bodies of water.

LATIN — *Ecce Romani, Books 1 and 2* (16) OR *Latin I* BY FR. ROBERT HENLE (20)

These books carry on from the base you have built over the last few years. They move slowly, with plenty of opportunity for practice. There are many support materials: tests and key, workbook and key, text translation.

The drawback to this text is that the keys are only available to licensed teachers. I found a cooperative Christian school to order my materials for me.

You could use the Fr. Henle text. If you wish to achieve a certain level of competence in Latin and then go on to a modern language, or concentrate on other subjects, that is probably the thing to do. If, however, you wish to stay with Latin for all of high school, in preparation for college Latin, you should wait for Fr. Henle so that you don't find yourself in the last year without a text.

ART — *Art Smart!* BY SUSAN RODRIGUEZ (17) OR ANY OF THE PREVIOUS YEARS SUGGESTIONS

This program can be used for many years. I suggested it last year; it could be used for three years easily. *Art Smart!* features a hands on approach to art appreciation. There are 40 slides of works of art and lesson plans to go with each one. The lessons include information about the artist and directions for producing a similar work. All needed materials are listed.

MUSIC — *Music Smart!* BY GWEN HOTCHKISS (17)

This is also a text that is useful at many different levels, and can be used for a number of years. As I said earlier, *Music Smart!* comes with three tapes of music and complete lesson plans.

## TENTATIVE SCHEDULE FOR EIGHTH GRADE

| MON. | TUE. | WED. | THURS. | FRI. |
|------|------|------|--------|------|
| MATH | MATH | MATH | MATH | MATH |
| ENGLISH | ENGLISH | ENGLISH | ENGLISH | LITERATURE |
| LATIN | LATIN | LATIN | LATIN | MUSIC |
| RELIGION | ART | RELIGION | RELIGION | HISTORY |
| SCIENCE | SCIENCE | SCIENCE | SCIENCE | |
| | HISTORY | GEOGRAPHY | | |

HISTORY READING AND WRITING TO BE DONE IN THE EVENING OR ON FRIDAY

# GRADE EIGHT RESOURCE LISTS

## RELIGION STUDY GUIDE FOR EIGHTH GRADE—
## THE CASE FOR CHRISTIANITY

### PART I, CHAPTER 1

C.S. Lewis makes two points in the first section. What are they? Which common way of behaving supports the first point and which the second?

### PART I, CHAPTER 2

In this section Lewis begins by giving three arguments to prove something about the Moral Law. What is he trying to establish?

Then he gives two reasons for thinking that the Law of Human Nature (or Moral Law) is a real truth (like math) not a convention (like traffic laws). What are the two reasons?

Do you understand the final point he makes about distinguishing between differences of morality and differences of belief about facts?

### PART I, CHAPTER 3

What makes the "Law of Human Nature," different from the laws of nature?

What examples show that the Moral Law (what a man ought to do) is different from what is convenient or profitable? Give two examples.

Summarize Lewis' summary, that is, list the points he has made about the Moral Law.

a) Men ought to be

b) The Moral Law is not a

c) The Moral Law is not a

d) The Moral Law is not a

e) Therefore,

PART 1, CHAPTER 4

Copy the sentence in the first paragraph that best states what has been established by Lewis' reasoning so far.

What, roughly, are the two views of how the universe came to be? Can science answer the question, "Why is there a universe?"

If there is a power behind the things that are, that creates them and directs them, where would we look for evidence of it?

What three names does Lewis give for the in-between view he mentions in the note?

PART 1, CHAPTER 5

When do you make progress by going back?

What are the two "bits of evidence" we have, without the Bible, about the Somebody behind the Moral Law?

Why is the second bit of evidence better?

How have we made ourselves the enemies of the Somebody who made the Moral Law?

PART 2, CHAPTER 1

How is a Christian more tolerant of other religions than an atheist?

Why is it that an atheist, who does not believe that the universe or anything in it was designed by Someone on purpose, cannot trust his own thinking to be true?

The first division of humanity is into those who believe in God and those who do not. Of those who believe in God, the next division is between the sort of God they believe in. What two sorts are there?

Why is Christianity a fighting religion?

How does the injustice of the world prove that there must be a God?

PART 2, CHAPTER 2

What is the Christian explanation of "a universe that contains much that is obviously bad and meaningless, but containing creatures who know it is bad and meaningless"?

If we distinguish between a Good Power and a Bad Power in the universe, what third thing do we need to judge which is which?

Since Christianity is not Dualism, how does it explain the existence of a dark power?

## PART 2, CHAPTER 3

What did God give us that made it possible for the world to have evil in it?

What was the sin of Satan, and the sin he taught to us?

What three things (before Jesus' coming) did God do to counteract the evil Satan did?

What three claims of Christ were "talking as if he was God"?

## PART 2, CHAPTER 4

What did Jesus come mainly to do?

If it is necessary to have a complete understanding of Christ's sacrifice, what is necessary to be believed?

What is the "catch" in repentance?

## PART 2, CHAPTER 5

What three things spread Christ's life to us?

What does "believing things on authority" mean?

If we receive the Christ-life by these three things, why are we obliged to do anything else?

The Christian doesn't think God will love us because we're good, but that ...

# LITERATURE LIST FOR EIGHTH GRADE

| | |
|---|---|
| *Pride and Prejudice* | JANE AUSTEN |
| *Death Comes for the Archbishop* | WILLA CATHER |
| *Father Brown* SERIES | G.K. CHESTERTON |
| *Two Years Before the Mast* | R.H. DANA |

| | |
|---|---|
| *Sherlock Holmes* SERIES | SIR ARTHUR CONAN DOYLE |
| *The White Company* | SIR ARTHUR CONAN DOYLE |
| *The Kitchen Madonna* | RUMER GODDEN |
| *In This House of Brede* | RUMER GODDEN |
| *Riders of the Purple Sage* | ZANE GRAY |
| *All Creatures Great and Small* | JAMES HERRIOT |
| *Prisoner of Zenda* | ANTHONY HOPE |
| *Tom Brown's School Days* | THOMAS HUGHES |
| *Tom Brown at Oxford* | THOMAS HUGHES |
| *The Narnian Chronicles* | C.S. LEWIS |
| *Out of the Silent Planet* | C.S. LEWIS |
| *Perelandra* | C.S. LEWIS |
| *That Hideous Strength* | C.S. LEWIS |
| *Ivanhoe* | SIR WALTER SCOTT |
| *The Hobbit* | J.R.R. TOLKIEN |
| *The Lord of the Rings* | J.R.R. TOLKIEN |
| *Around the World in Eighty Days* | JULES VERNE |
| *Journey to the Center of the Earth* | JULES VERNE |
| *Twenty Thousand Leagues Under the Sea* | JULES VERNE |

## POETRY LIST FOR EIGHTH GRADE

| | |
|---|---|
| "HORATIUS" | THOMAS LORD MACAULAY |
| "ON FIRST LOOKING INTO CHAPMAN'S HOMER" | JOHN KEATS |
| "THE SPLENDOR FALLS ON CASTLE WALLS" | ALFRED LORD TENNYSON |
| "THE LADY OF SHALLOT" | ALFRED LORD TENNYSON |
| "LOCHNIVAR" | SIR WALTER SCOTT |
| EXCERPTS FROM "THE IDYLLS OF THE KING" | ALFRED LORD TENNYSON |

## SHAKESPEARE

| | |
|---|---|
| *Macbeth* | ACT V, v, 1-36 |

"TOMORROW, AND TOMORROW, AND TOMORROW, CREEPS IN THIS PETTY PACE FROM DAY TO DAY, ..."

| | | |
|---|---|---|
| *The Merchant of Venice* | ACT IV, I, 178-224 | |

"THE QUALITY OF MERCY IS NOT STRAIN'D."

| | | |
|---|---|---|
| *The Merchant of Venice* | ACT V, I, 33-77 | |

"HOW SWEET THE MOONLIGHT SLEEPS UPON THIS BANK!"

SONNETS XVIII, XIX, XXX, XXXVI, CXVI, CXXXVIII

## HISTORY READING LIST FOR EIGHTH GRADE— MEDIEVAL HISTORY

Used as supplements to *The Old World and America* by Fr. Philip Furlong (Chapters V-IX).

An "L" after the author's name indicates that the library or used book sources will be your best bet for securing this title, "IP" indicates that the book is currently in print, "*" indicates an especially enjoyable book. If a book belongs to an identifiable series I will indicate that by using one of the following abbreviations: VB — Vision Book (Catholic), AMB — American Background Book (Catholic), LKB — Landmark Book (Christian orientation), SB — Signature Book, NSB — North Star Book, CL — Clarion Book (Catholic), WWTB — We Were There Book.

| | | |
|---|---|---|
| *Augustine Comes to Kent* | BARBARA WILLARD | L, * CL |
| *Fingal's Quest* | MADELEINE POLLAND | L, * CL |
| *The King's Thane* | CHARLES BRADY | L, * CL |
| *Son of Charlemagne* | BARBARA WILLARD | L, * CL |
| *Mission to Cathay* | MADELEINE POLLAND | L, * CL |
| *If All the Swords in England* | BARBARA WILLARD | L, * CL |
| *The Two Trumpeters of Vienna* | HERTHA PAULI | L, * CL |
| *A Trumpet Sounds* | HENRY GARNETT | L, * CL |
| *The Blue Gonfalon* | MARGARET HUBBARD | L, * CL |
| *Where Valour Lies* | ADELE AND CATEAU DELEEUW | L, * CL |
| *William the Conqueror* | THOMAS B. COSTAIN | L, * LKB |
| *Man with a Sword* | HENRY TREECE | L, * |
| *Swords from the North* | HENRY TREECE | L, * |
| *Song of Roland* | (UNKNOWN) | L, |
| *Castle* | DAVID MACAULAY | IP, * |

| | | |
|---|---|---|
| *Idylls of the King* | ALFRED LORD TENNYSON | IP, * |
| *Ivanhoe* | SIR WALTER SCOTT | IP, * |
| *Young Folk's History of England* | CHARLOTTE YONGE | L |
| *The Door in the Wall* | MARGUERITE DE ANGELI | IP, * |
| *Cathedral* | DAVID MACAULAY | IP, * |
| *Boy Knight of Reims* | ELOISE LOWNSBERY | L |
| *Joy in Stone* | SABRA HOLBROOK | L |
| *St. Dominic and the Rosary* | CATHERINE BEEBE | L, * VB |
| *Francis and Clare, Saints of Assisi* | HELEN HOMAN | IP, * VB |
| *St. Thomas Aquinas and the Preaching Beggars* | BRENDAN LARNEN, O.P. AND MILTON LOMASK | L, * VB |
| *The Crusaders* | A.J. CHURCH | L |
| *The Crusades* | ANTHONY WEST | L, LKB |
| *We Were There with Richard the Lionhearted* | ROBERT WEBB | L, WWTB |
| *St. Louis and the Last Crusade* | MARGARET HUBBARD | L, * VB |
| *King Arthur and His Knights* | THOMAS MALORY | IP, * |
| *Castles* | LADYBIRD BOOK | L |
| *The Story of a Castle* | JOHN GOODALL | IP |
| *Sir Gawain and the Green Knight* | J.R.R. TOLKIEN | IP, * |
| *Otto of the Silver Hand* | HOWARD PYLE | IP, * |
| *Looking into the Middle Ages* | HUCK SCARRY | L |
| *Spice Ho! A Story of Discovery* | AGNES HEWES | L |
| *The Travels of Marco Polo* (VARIOUS EDITIONS) | MARCO POLO | IP |
| *Ghengis Kahn and the Mongol Horde* | HAROLD LAMB | L, LKB |
| *The Bayeaux Tapestry* | NORMAN DENNY AND JOSEPHINE FILMER-SANKEY | IP, * |
| *The Age of Chivalry* | NATIONAL GEOGRAPHIC | IP |
| *The War of the Roses* | ELIZABETH HALLAM | IP |
| *The Plantagenet Chronicles* | ELIZABETH HALLAM | IP |
| *Four Gothic Kings* | ELIZABETH HALLAM | IP |

| | | |
|---|---|---|
| *Fifteen Decisive Battles of the World* | EDWARD CREASY | IP,* |
| *Life of St. Joan* | LOUIS DE WOHL | L,* VB |
| *In the Days of King Hal* | MARION TAGGERT | L,* |
| *The Fall of Constantinople* | BERNADINE KIELTY | L, LKB |
| *The Trumpeter of Krakow* | ERIC KELLY | IP,* |
| *Master Skylark* | JOHN BENNET | IP,* |
| *The Life of Thomas More* | WILLIAM ROPER | IP,* |
| *A Proud Tale of Minerva and Scarlet* | E.L. KONIGSBURG | IP,* |
| *The Golden Book of the Renaissance* | (GOLDEN PRESS) | L |
| *Adam of the Road* | ELIZABETH GRAY | IP,* |
| *St. George and the Dragon* | MARGARET HODGES | IP,* |
| *Beowulf* | IAN SERRAILLIER | IP,* |
| *Canterbury Tales* | BARBARA COHEN | IP,* |
| *Jackaroo* | CYNTHIA VOIGT | IP |
| *The Black Arrow* | ROBERT LOUIS STEVENSON | IP, |
| *The Adventures of Robin Hood* | ROGER LANCELYN GREEN | IP, |
| *The Merry Adventures of Robin Hood* | HOWARD PYLE | IP,* |
| *King Arthur and His Knights of the Round Table* | ROGER LANCELYN GREEN | IP,* |
| *The Story of the Grail and the Passing of Arthur* | HOWARD PYLE | IP,* |
| *I, Juan De Pareja* | ELIZABETH BORTEN DE TREVINO | IP,* |
| *Don Quixote and Sancho Panza* | MARGARET HODGES | IP,* |

## HISTORY DATES LIST FOR EIGHTH GRADE

| | | |
|---|---|---|
| (A.D.) | 529 | ST. BENEDICT ESTABLISHES MONASTERY AT MONTE CASSINO, ITALY. |
| | 529 | EMPEROR JUSTINIAN ISSUES *Codex Justinianus* |
| | 550 | KING ARTHUR REIGNS IN ENGLAND. |

598    POPE GREGORY I (THE GREAT) SENDS AUGUSTINE TO ENGLAND.

622    MOHAMMED MAKES "HEJIRA" TO MEDINA.

732    CHARLES THE HAMMER STOPS THE MOSLEM ADVANCE AT TOURS.

800    CHARLEMAGNE CROWNED HOLY ROMAN EMPEROR BY POPE LEO III.

886    ALFRED THE GREAT DRIVES THE DANES FROM WESSEX.

1066    DUKE WILLIAM OF NORMANDY CONQUERS SAXON ENGLAND.

1099    FIRST CRUSADE TAKES JERUSALEM.

1146    LOUIS VII AND CONRAD III "TAKE THE CROSS"— SECOND CRUSADE.

1187    SALADIN RECAPTURES JERUSALEM.

1192    RICHARD THE LION-HEART AND SALADIN MAKE TRUCE TO END THE THIRD CRUSADE.

1204    FOURTH CRUSADE SACKS CONSTANTINOPLE.

1208    ST. FRANCIS FOUNDS THE FRANCISCAN FRIARS.

1215    MAGNA CARTA SIGNED BY KING JOHN.

1270    ST. LOUIS (KING LOUIS IX) DIES ON CRUSADE.

1272    ST. THOMAS AQUINAS STOPS WORK ON THE SUMMA THEOLOGIAE.

1295    MARCO POLO RETURNS TO VENICE FROM CHINA AND THE COURT OF KUBLAI KAHN.

1321    DANTE DIES.

1346    BATTLE OF CRECY — EDWARD III AND HIS LONGBOWS VICTORIOUS.

1348    THE BLACK DEATH DEVASTATES EUROPE.

1415    HENRY V OF ENGLAND WINS BATTLE OF AGINCOURT IN NORMANDY.

1429    JOAN OF ARC RELIEVES ORLEANS.

1453    FALL OF CONSTANTINOPLE

1453    END OF THE HUNDRED YEARS WAR BETWEEN ENGLAND AND FRANCE.

1492    COLUMBUS DISCOVERS THE NEW WORLD.

# GEOGRAPHY LIST FOR EIGHTH GRADE— EUROPEAN CAPITALS AND THEIR RIVERS

| Capital City | Country | River or Sea | Empties Into |
|---|---|---|---|
| ROME | ITALY | TIBER | TYRRHENIAN SEA |
| PARIS | FRANCE | SEINE | ENGLISH CHANNEL |
| LONDON | GREAT BRITAIN | THAMES | NORTH SEA |
| VIENNA | AUSTRIA | DANUBE | BLACK SEA |
| WARSAW | POLAND | VISTULA | BALTIC SEA |
| BERLIN | GERMANY | SPREE | ELBE |
| ATHENS | GREECE | AEGEAN SEA | MEDITERRANEAN SEA |
| CONSTANTINOPLE (ISTANBUL) | TURKEY | BOSPORUS STRAIT | SEA OF MARMARA |
| LISBON | PORTUGAL | TAGUS | ATLANTIC OCEAN |
| MADRID | SPAIN | TRIBUTARY OF TAGUS | TAGUS |
| MOSCOW | RUSSIA | OKA | VOLGA |

# Ninth Grade Curriculum

**Sources for items followed by a number in parentheses may be found at the back of the book under the suppliers list.**

RELIGION — *Chief Truths of the Faith* BY FR. JOHN LAUX (14), *Catholic Morality* BY FR. JOHN LAUX (14)

These texts cover systematically and thoughtfully the doctrine of the Catholic Church regarding her chief teachings. The lessons include well chosen questions requiring careful analysis. The writing assignments are particularly good because they help the student do just what he should be doing at this stage of development: present a cogent, well-reasoned argument. The questions in the text lead the student through the argument so that he can see it clearly and then reproduce it.

I also recommend reviewing the Ten Commandments, Eight Beatitudes, and Gifts and Fruits of the Holy Spirit.

MATHEMATICS — *Algebra I* (SAXON) (3)

This text introduces the next level of algebraic skills. It presents the material in an orderly manner and reviews the concepts regularly. If the student does the lessons consistently and completely, redoing any problems that have been done incorrectly, he will be able to work through this text.

There is a solutions manual available that will help you help your child through any tough problems.

GRAMMAR AND COMPOSITION — *Warriner's English Grammar and Composition, Third Course* (19), PAPERS IN HISTORY

Grammar and writing exercises should be done regularly. Papers in History, English and Religion will be occasions for practicing writing skills, as well as writing exercises from this text. The text covers skills used in compositions, summaries, reports and stories. It also reviews basic grammar and spelling.

Work diligently on re-writing. It is better to do a few papers well than to do many papers poorly. Even one paper carefully done, with real attention to constructing a reasoned argument, will do more to teach a child how to learn, how to communicate, and how to think than any number of sloppy efforts.

SPELLING AND VOCABULARY — *Warriner's English Grammar and Composition, Third Course* (19)

Warriner's has a chapter for review of spelling "demons." It doesn't take long to review this section, and it can be done as a short separate unit at the beginning of the year. If your child is a good speller you could skip this part of the text.

LITERATURE — *Catholic Readings in American Literature* (20) *or* ATTACHED LITERATURE LIST

Whether you choose to enroll with Seton for this course or use the list I include at the end of this chapter, it is important that you discuss the readings with your child. This will continue to be true throughout high school, but it is particularly important in this first year when there is a transition from the dialectical phase of the Trivium to the rhetorical. It involves difficult material considered both in the light of the argument of the author and the means he employs to make that argument. There are subtle considerations to be made, more subtle than the child has been used to making. For example, most children will need help in identifying the irony that leads to a conclusion which, on the face of it, is opposed to the reasoning process. The context will play more of a role than it has previously in understanding the author's way of proceeding. This kind of consideration needs adult guidance, at least initially.

Many of the Seton English high school courses are excellent. The syllabus for this class contains discussion questions as well as directed study plans. And the material in the course will supplement your history readings by adding a needed Catholic perspective.

The reason I include a literature list as an alternative is that the Seton course is very demanding, more demanding than may be suitable for your child at this point. This is not a question of intelligence but of development. When you commit yourself to this course you are committing yourself to a great deal of work, and the loss of the flexibility that you have had up to this point. You can't say with the same ease as before, "I don't think you need to work on this part of the text, so skip it and do the next." You can still say it, but since there are, reasonably enough, certain exercises that are requirements for finishing the course, if you do make that decision, your child may not complete that particular course.

The literature list at the end of this chapter includes readings that I have used successfully with a number of high school students. They are both readable and discussable at this level. I have found that alternating novels and short stories works quite well. Our discussions have centered on plot, characterization, theme, setting, and devices such as irony and inference.

All through the high school courses we have found it helpful, though not necessary, to have more than one student for discussions. Discussions benefit from a variety of viewpoints.

Once again, the books that you choose to read and discuss with your child should not be the only books he reads. The books on my list are books that children of this age often enjoy. Introduce your child to them and let him read whenever there is time. Have the books where they are easily available, and try to establish a regular reading time. In our house everyone reads after dinner until bed time.

## POETRY — SEE LIST

The study of poetry should include analysis. Use the sonnets that were memorized last year as material for analysis. Have your child write out in prose what the sonnet says in verse. Analyze the meter and pattern of the sonnets. Perhaps your child could try his hand at writing one.

I have included some other suggestions in the list at the end of this section. Compare different poems and talk about their differences. Is there a mood created in the poem? What is it and how does the author produce it? At this stage it is more important for the student to think carefully about the poem than to see every literary device it contains. One actually learns more by working on understanding the poem, than by having someone else explain, too soon, all the poem contains and how it achieves its effects. In the Seton English courses for 10th through 12th grades these literary devices are discussed. This year the student should notice what he can about poetry on his own.

SCIENCE — *Earth Science* (20) (TEXT—*Earth Science for Christian Schools* BY BOB JONES UNIVERSITY PRESS)

This Seton Science course has a number of worthwhile supplements, in addition to the text. The text is available directly from the publisher, but the supplements included by Seton makes it worthwhile purchasing this course through Seton. The syllabus presents facts about Galileo, and his problems with the Catholic Church, that counteract certain assertions in the text itself. The text is quite good in its presentation of geologic material, but the supplements are important to balance a few religious errors in it. There is also a stimulating discussion of evolution using *The World That Perished,* a presentation of the creationist point of view.

The written work required of the student entails the presentation of a reasoned argument and the collating and summarizing of material from different sources. It is a good example of the practice of the method of dialectic on a well chosen subject matter.

HISTORY — *The March of Democracy* BY JOHN TRUSLOW ADAMS (7), *The World's Great Speeches* (DOVER PRESS) (1)

*The March of Democracy* is out of print, but it is pretty widely available in used book stores; evidently it was popular at one time. It has a fairly lengthy, but very readable account of American history from the revolution to World War II. If you are unable to find this work, look for another older account of American history.

Then assign, over the course of the year, three substantial papers of about 1,500 words. I have included a list of possible topics, and I recommend that each paper have a different approach to the chosen topic.

Such approaches include first person descriptions of the time read about as though you were living at the time (Washington's description of the war, for example), the pros and cons of a particular question (Was the North correct in insisting that the South could not secede?), the imagined recorded conversation between two important characters from history (Jay and Madison discussing limited government), and narrative essays.

Toward the end of the year use *Great Speeches* for practice in dialectic. Have your child read a speech from a period in history that is of interest to him. Have him outline it, lay the outline aside and a few days later use that outline to reproduce the speech to the best of his ability. Have him jumble the order of the outline, lay it aside, and then later try to reduce the confusion to the best possible order. Comparing his finished work with the original, a student will discover faults and amend them. Shorter speeches are better for beginners, and familiarity with the issues raised in the speech is an asset for such a project.

Even if this is your first year homeschooling I think this approach will work well. Any gaps in historical knowledge can be filled in later.

## LATIN — *Ecce Romani, Books 3, 4, and 5* (16) OR *Latin II* BY FR. ROBERT HENLE (20)

In either case these books continue the program from last year. Work through the text, following the internal order. *Ecce Romani* has many support materials. Fr. Henle's text is very good. For a description see tenth grade.

If you are beginning Latin for the first time I recommend using *Latin I* by Fr. Henle. Plan to use it over the next two years, working through each lesson throughly. Fr. Henle's texts are out of print, so if you wish to use them you will need to go through Seton or Our Lady of the Rosary. Occasionally they will turn up in used book stores, but you would still need the answer keys.

## ART/MUSIC — VARIOUS WORKS IN BOTH CATEGORIES

Your student will be busier this year than in past years, and he already has, hopefully, a foundation in both of these subjects which will lead him to pursue them on his own. For these reasons I do not include either art and music on a regular basis in my ninth grade curriculum. So far, in our house, it hasn't been necessary.

It is worthwhile, however, to spend some time talking about the dialectic of works of art. There is a *quasi* argument in a painting; the artist wishes you to see something he sees, in the way that he sees it. Talk about how he accomplishes that. Your student has, at this point, a wide acquaintance with artists and their pictures. He also knows something about technique. Use that information in such a discussion.

If you are just beginning to homeschool, see earlier years for suggestions.

## Typing — *Typing Tutor* (2)

If your child does not yet type it is a good idea to learn now. I realize that this is not a part of a classical curriculum, but it helps to read typed papers rather than handwritten ones!

There are many alternatives to *Typing Tutor*, both other educational computer programs and books that can be used with a typewriter. The basic point is to learn to type. Mary Pride discusses many computer programs in her *Big Book of Home Learning*.

## Tentative Schedule for Ninth Grade

| Mon. | Tues. | Wed. | Thurs. | Fri. |
|------|-------|------|--------|------|
| Math | Math | Math | Math | Math |
| English | English | English | English | English |
| Latin | Latin | Latin | Latin | History |
| Religion | Religion | Religion | Religion | |
| Science | Science | Science | Science | |

History Reading to be done in the evening or on Friday

# GRADE NINE RESOURCE LISTS

## LITERATURE LIST FOR NINTH GRADE

| | |
|---|---|
| *The Virginian* | OWEN WISTER |
| *Jane Eyre* | CHARLOTTE BRONTE |
| *Wuthering Heights* | EMILY BRONTE |
| *Tom Sawyer* | MARK TWAIN |
| *Red Badge of Courage* | STEPHEN CRANE |
| *The Deerslayer* | JAMES F. COOPER |
| *Oliver Twist* | CHARLES DICKENS |
| *Silas Marner* | GEORGE ELIOT |
| *Lorna Doone* | RICHARD BLACKMORE |

### ALTERNATIVES

| | |
|---|---|
| *The Scarlet Letter* | NATHANIEL HAWTHORNE |
| *The House of the Seven Gables* | NATHANIEL HAWTHORNE |
| *Huckleberry Finn* | MARK TWAIN |
| *Great Expectations* | CHARLES DICKENS |
| *A Tale of Two Cities* | CHARLES DICKENS |
| *David Copperfield* | CHARLES DICKENS |
| *Kidnapped* | ROBERT L. STEVENSON |
| *Treasure Island* | ROBERT L. STEVENSON |
| *The Count of Monte Cristo* | ALEXANDER DUMAS |
| *Mutiny on the Bounty* | CHARLES NORDOFF AND JAMES NORMAN HALL |
| *Les Miserables* | VICTOR HUGO |
| *Death Comes for the Archbishop* | WILLA CATHER |
| *Shadows on the Rock* | WILLA CATHER |
| "THE PROPHECY OF SOCRATES" | PLATO |
| "THE DEATH OF SOCRATES" | PLATO |
| SELECTIONS FROM *The Autobiography of Benjamin Franklin* | |

### SHORT STORIES

| | |
|---|---|
| "THE LUCK OF ROARING CAMP" | BRET HARTE |
| "THE RANSOM OF RED CHIEF" | O. HENRY |
| "THE GIFT OF THE MAGI" | O. HENRY |

| | |
|---|---|
| "The Retrieved Reformation" | O. Henry |
| "Little Bo-Peep" | O. Henry |
| "The Devil and Daniel Webster" | Stephen V. Benet |
| "Rip Van Winkle" | Washington Irving |
| "The Legend of Sleepy Hollow" | Washington Irving |
| "The Most Dangerous Game" | Richard Connell |
| "The Secret Life of Walter Mitty" | James Thurber |
| "Dr. Jekyll and Mr. Hyde" | Robert L. Stevenson |
| "Neighbor Rosicky" | Willa Cather |
| "The Great Stone Face" | Nathaniel Hawthorne |

## Poetry List and Other Works to Memorize

| | |
|---|---|
| "The Daffodils" | William Wordsworth |
| The Second Inaugural Address | Abraham Lincoln |
| "The Flute" | Wilfrid Gibson |
| "Lepanto" | G.K. Chesterton |
| "A Thing of Beauty" | John Keats |
| "The Day is Done" | Longfellow |
| *Sonnets from the Portuguese* | E.B. Browning |
| "When I was One and Twenty" | A.E. Housman |
| "Love" | George Herbert |
| "The Pulley" | George Herbert |
| "Evangeline" | Henry Wadsworth Longfellow |

## List of History Questions for Ninth Grade

1. Why was the Revolutionary War fought? Consider the course of the negotiations between the colonists and England. How did the Stamp Act, the Tea Tax and other ordinances from England affect the decision of the colonists? How does this compare to the revolution in France?

2. America is said to have a tradition of limited government. Show from the Constitution what some of those limits are. Is this idea of government found in the Declaration of Independence? Can government aim at making men good and happy and still be limited?

3. Why does the U.S. have both state and national governments? How did this arrangement arise at the Constitutional Convention? It is generally agreed that the states have lost power over time. Do you think that this is true? If so, discuss two cases where the change took place.

4. What was the Civil War fought about? Consider the status of slavery in the Constitution, its relation to the Declaration of Independence, the Northwest Ordinance, the Compromises of 1820 and 1850, the Dred Scott Decision, Lincoln's career, and the outcome of the war, including the 13th and 15th amendments.

5. Write about an important figure in American history. Consider both his character — virtues and vices — and his effects for good or ill on society at large.

6. The U.S. experienced massive immigration from 1900-1920. Discuss the immigrants' reasons for coming, the problems they met and the question of "Americanization" of the newcomers. What special advantages did Catholics have and what difficulties did they meet?

7. What is an income tax? Why did the Constitution have to be amended to allow one? What are the reasons for and against such a mode of taxation? How have the rates changed over the period 1911-1945? How do they compare to present rates?

8. What was the grand strategy of the Allies in World War II? Select and discuss several key decisions American leaders had to make, and evaluate their decisions. Examples might be: use of the A bomb, timing and location of D-Day, invasion of Italy, the "Germany first" decision, island hopping in the Pacific, strategic bombing of Germany. Use Catholic principles about war, and the tactics of war in such an evaluation.

9. After the stock market crash of 1929 the country experienced an economic crisis called the "Great Depression." Describe the seriousness and depth of the depression and the response of the so-called "New Deal." Discuss the policy, including its constitutionality. (See especially Article I, section 8 in the Constitution and Federalist 41.)

# NOTES

# The
# Rhetorical
# Stage

# The Rhetorical Stage

THE FINAL STAGE OF THE TRIVIUM, the rhetorical, overlaps with the dialectical on one end and the movement to subjects as subjects, rather than practice for the method proper to a stage of development, on the other. It seems to be characterized in the student both by the discovery he needs to know more, and a resulting interest in and capacity for acquiring information. The imagination is active; there is a new enjoyment of the poetical, in literature, music and art.

This combination of information and poetical interests gives the student an ability, which our curriculum must foster, to express himself in elegant and persuasive language.

Miss Sayers, in her essay, says of students at this stage that "The doors of the storehouse of knowledge should now be thrown open for them to browse about as they will. The things once learned by rote will be seen in new contexts; the things once coldly analyzed can now be brought together to form a new synthesis; here and there a sudden insight will bring about that most exciting of all discoveries: the realization that a truism is true ... Any child who already shows a disposition to specialize should be given his head: for, when the use of the tools has been well and truly learned, it is available for any study whatever."

In practice these considerations have at least two consequences that must be taken into account. One is that the manner of expression of ideas now has central importance in the curriculum. There are exercises that can contribute to elegant writing. I have mentioned some in the latter part of the ninth grade History curriculum. The best way, however, to improve writing skills is to write with attention to clarity, elegance and persuasion. Then re-write, cut down, rephrase, and re-write again. This takes time.

The other consequence also involves time. If your child is to be "given his head," allowed to specialize, he is going to need time to do it.

For these reasons I do not recommend simply buying a complete high school curriculum and using it in all its parts. They all take too much time to finish. I know many homeschoolers across the country and I do not know of one who has been able to finish all the required activities for a school year in a year. Of course that doesn't mean there aren't any, but it is significant that so many people are not able to do so.

This is a problem not just because it is discouraging, and disruptive of family life, but because it does not allow the child to develop the faculties he should be developing at this stage. To do that he needs time.

Having said that, I nevertheless do recommend many of the individual Seton High School courses. This is because they are outstanding. They require time, but in the courses I recommend much of the time spent is spent on activities that are consonant with the goals of our curriculum. I recommend, and so does Seton, that you look over the syllabus of each class at the beginning of the year and decide what you are going to have your student do. There are a certain number of required exercises that must be sent in each quarter. I have my students concentrate on those and fit other suggestions around them.

It is possible to take the Seton High School courses individually, without enrolling in every class. In my ninth grade curriculum I recommend the Seton Earth Science Course, even though there are no other Seton courses in my curriculum at that point. Later grades have many more Seton courses recommended. You may also take individual courses at your local high school or junior college, a serious consideration for those who want science laboratories in their curriculum.

You will notice that the course descriptions in the upcoming years are brief, and that I no longer include supplementary lists for the various grades.

There are two reasons for this, one of which I have already mentioned. The rhetorical stage is more determined by the student's interests, and the parents *guidance*, than has previously been true. It is characterized by the student's spirit of inquiry. *He* needs to decide what to inquire about. Additionally, the materials included in the courses are themselves more substantial, and already contain many resources.

If you decide to continue with your own curriculum through high school, you will need to keep records for college applications. The records should list the course, the grade for each quarter, the cumulative grade for the course all in one line. After all courses and grades are listed, there should be a grade point average for the year and cumulative grade point average listed.

# Tenth Grade Curriculum

**Sources for items followed by a number in parentheses may be found at the back of the book under the suppliers list.**

RELIGION — *The Mass and the Sacraments* BY FR. JOHN LAUX (14), *Catholic Apologetics* BY FR. JOHN LAUX (14)

These texts both contain serious studies of their subject matter. The lessons include well chosen questions requiring careful analysis. The writing assignments are good, as they were in the previous texts. But because of the writing required in the other courses this year, you should assign the written work sparingly. Instead, discuss these texts with your child. Theology is the most important subject in the curriculum; it is worth the time it takes to prepare for the discussion. Additionally, since the chapters are not long, it is not as hard to keep on top of the readings as it might be in some of the other classes.

MATHEMATICS — *Algebra 2* BY SAXON (3)

This text continues the study of algebra. It presents the material in an orderly manner and reviews the concepts regularly. As in the last text, if the student does the lessons consistently and completely, re-doing any problems that have been done incorrectly, he will be able to work through this text. The homeschool packet comes with tests and I recommend doing a certain number of them to check on the mastery level of the student. Sometimes students answer the more difficult questions by referring back to the text. Then they think they understand something they don't. The tests will reveal such a situation.

There is a solutions manual available that will help you help your child through any tough problems.

## ENGLISH — *English 10* (20)

*English 10* is a composition and literature analysis course. Some part of every quarter is spent on writing skills. The text used is the Warriner's Grammar and Composition Fourth Course. Paragraph writing, longer compositions and how to write a research paper are all studied. The other part of each quarter concentrates on literary analysis. *Animal Farm* and *A Tale of Two Cities* are both investigated with a view to theme, character development and conflict. There is a section on poetry analysis as well that studies imagery, figures of speech and other poetical devices. We particularly enjoyed the discussion of *Animal Farm.*

While you could purchase and use these texts without going through Seton, the material in the syllabus is very helpful. I am very glad that we took this course through Seton.

## LITERATURE — *Catholic Readings in World Literature* (20)

This course uses a Catholic textbook, which contains Catholic selections and information from a Catholic point of view. It also has a number of delightful readings. This text, *Catholic Readings for High School,* is not available except through Seton, and even through them is only available as a rental.

## SCIENCE — *Biology* (20) (TEXT — *God's Living Creation*, PUBLISHED BY BOB JONES UNIVERSITY PRESS)

This Seton Science course, like last year's, has a number of worthwhile supplements. The syllabus is important because it presents the Catholic position on evolution in a very well reasoned article, and has the student read the encyclical *Humani Generis,* and *The Origin and Early History of Man* by Fr. Patrick O'Connell. The question of euthanasia is also discussed and the encyclical, *Declaration on Euthanasia,* is read.

The text itself uses technical language, but the material presented is interesting.

The written work required of the student entails the presentation of reasoned arguments and the collating and summarizing of material from different sources.

HISTORY — *A History of the English Speaking Peoples* BY WINSTON CHURCHILL (7), *How the Reformation Happened* BY HILAIRE BELLOC (1), AND *The Beginning of the English Reformation* BY HUGH ROSS WILLIAMSON (NEUMANN PRESS) (1)

A wide historical acquaintance supplies the student with knowledge of two sorts. On the one hand certain causes of the present political and social order come to light. The Constitution of the United States, for example, did not spring into being from nothingness. There was a tradition, a way of thinking, that was formed in England prior to the revolution. A study of English history illuminates American history.

The other kind of knowledge that history contributes to is universal, and is itself of two sorts. The necessary experience for political prudence is lacking in the young, but reading thoughtful historical works will in some measure supply that experience. Thus, a consideration of history prepares the student for the study of both ethics and politics. Even an understanding of the soul and the nature of man is clarified by the examples of history.

For these reasons it is profitable to read Churchill's *History of the English Speaking People*. It illuminates our history, and it prepares the student for philosophy.

I recommend that the student write short summaries of every fifty pages or so, for the sake of reinforcement and review. The bulk of the writing in this year is in the English and Literature program, and you want your child to concentrate on making those as well written as he can.

LATIN — *Latin I* BY FR. ROBERT HENLE (20)

*Latin I* is an excellent text. The student reviews the material he has already learned and moves on, from this foundation, to a more complex treatment of the subject. It is important to review vocabulary, and the Seton syllabus regularly urges such review. The tests are quite good, and the additional readings are very interesting. I have found that anticipating those tests is motivating for my children. This text does not move as quickly as some others I have used over the years and I like it better for that reason. The material seems to actually sink in permanently.

## Art/Music — Various works in both categories

The tenth grader should be encouraged to explore these areas on his own. If you have used some of the suggestions of previous years for art and music, your child probably already has favorite works. If he doesn't, you could look over some of those earlier ideas and use them now, as time permits.

## Tentative Schedule for Tenth Grade

| Mon. | Tues. | Wed. | Thurs. | Fri. |
|---|---|---|---|---|
| Math | Math | Math | Math | Math |
| English | English | English | English | English |
| Latin | Latin | Latin | Latin | History |
| Religion | Religion | Religion | Religion | |
| Science | Science | Science | Science | |

History reading and writing to be done in the evening or on Friday

# Eleventh Grade Curriculum

**Sources for items followed by a number in parentheses may be found at the back of the book under the suppliers list.**

RELIGION — *Religion 11* (20)

An Introduction to the Bible by Fr. John Laux is the basic text for this course. It is an excellent introduction to Scripture study. During the course of the year each book of the Bible is introduced by the text, read by the student, and commented on in the text. Both the textual introductions and the commentary are helpful. Additionally, the Seton syllabus contains wonderful supplemental materials on Mary as Mediatrix, and on the Suffering Servant.

MATHEMATICS — *Geometry* (20)

Geometry is one of the disciplines in the Quadrivium. It is a subject, something studied not as a tool for other disciplines but as an end in itself. Euclid is not easy to do at home. It is time intensive, both in terms of presenting the propositions and watching their presentation.

The geometry course offered by Seton is one alternative. It teaches the basic notions of geometry, and allows the student to practice geometrical argument. It is a simpler and much more accessible text than the Saxon *Advanced Math*. The highly technical approach of the Saxon text makes it difficult to use without expert help.

ENGLISH — *English 11* (20)

This course is even better than the very satisfactory *English 10*. Whoever wrote the lesson plans for this syllabus did a wonderful job. The texts used are interesting and enjoyable, and the discussion questions provided are thought provoking. More importantly, they are helpful in leading the student to a deeper understanding of the text.

Various kinds of literary selections are used during the year. The books *The Song at the Scaffold, The Scarlet Letter, Screwtape Letters* and *The Bridge of San Luis Rey* are read, as well as *The Ballad of the White Horse*, a narrative poem, and *A Man for All Seasons*, a play.

HISTORY — *A History of Medieval Spain* BY JOSEPH O'CALLAGHAN (1,7) OR *Philip II, Isabella of Spain, Characters of the Inquisition, Saint Teresa of Avila*, ALL BY WILLIAM THOMAS WALSH (14)

*A History of Medieval Spain* is a good, objective, Catholic text. Having read so much English history, a study of Catholic Spain from her point of view supplies a certain kind of balance.

This text might be hard to find, but it is in print. Walsh's books are also in print and do furnish a considerable amount of Spanish background. There is a larger time period covered in the text, but the context of Walsh's books provides much of the same information.

The study of Spanish history, from the Spanish point of view, modifies the picture of Europe that most students will have after reading English histories. For this reason I think this is a fruitful study. But this is an area where a particular student's interest should be taken into account. Warren Carroll has completed three volumes of a four volume set of the history of Christendom that could be an alternative.

There is also Fr. Phillip Hughes' history of the Church. If your child did not study ancient history in grade school, he could concentrate on that time period now. Let your child decide where he wants to turn his attention. But make use of this time to read real history — not diluted textbooks. Textbooks do not prepare the student for philosophy or give him political prudence.

This is a two year course. There is plenty of material for two years in the text I recommend. Further, the kind of careful, thoughtful, reflective reading that these texts require takes time.

If you think it helpful, assign a paper or two through the year, the topic to be chosen by the student. Evaluate the paper with respect to elegance of expression as well as content.

There are many good reasons for spending time teaching, and learning, history. History gives a sense of perspective. It supplies material for right judgment. It makes it possible to see the present in the light of the past, so that the part is seen in the light of the whole. Rightly done, as I said in the Introduction, I think history is a preparation for both philosophy and theology. It is a suitable matter for the student to practice his newly developing intellectual skills upon, and it supplies experience, inductions for the cultivation of judgment.

Your History course can accomplish all of these goals, but the materials you use are going to make a big difference in how well they are achieved. This is so important that I would like to tell you what I have learned about evaluating texts. Then if you prefer a different course of study than the one I have recommended you will know what to look for.

When you are evaluating materials for your curriculum, look for material that is not ideologically motivated. That is, you don't want something with "an axe to grind" a particular view of women, or oppression, or government, that colors all of the content. For those that object that all information is colored in some way, I can only say that I have seen big internal differences between texts.

When my oldest daughter wanted to do a study of Spanish history, we needed to locate texts to use. (You would be surprised at how hard it is to find good Spanish history texts.) We finally found three texts which we compared to one another. One of them saw all Spanish history from the viewpoint of the Muslims. It was so blatantly pro-Muslim that it invalidated the whole of the work. Every particular event mentioned in this text that was also mentioned in the others said that the Muslims were in the right and the Spanish Catholics were wrong. The other texts sometimes agreed with that judgment, but not often.

A good text will present original sources whenever possible, using material that was written close to the time of the events. It won't draw too many conclusions, leaving that exercise to the reader. When it does draw conclusions it will acknowledge that there are other positions possible but give reasons why this seems to be the best understanding of the events.

Paul Murray Kendall's *Richard the Third* is a good example of this kind. Mr. Kendall thinks Richard was a good guy, unlike the impression most people have. But he cites materials from the time of Richard, points to their inconsistency with the usual view of his conduct, suggests alternative understandings and acknowledges that this is not the only point of view. The reader can tell that he is being asked to consider the same material the author was considering; he is not simply given the author's judgment. To approach history that way the author must be more committed to the truth than to his own position, and he must recognize that such a subject can't be known the way the sciences can be.

A good text will also avoid egregious errors, like informing the reader that annulment is another name for divorce. Or that Philip II was said to be a chaste man, but since that is impossible, he must have had mistresses. Or that the Reformation was inspired by the fact that the Catholic Church chained up the Bible. All of these positions are statements that I have actually seen in so-called history books.

There are certain standard difficulties that texts often have. When checking out a text look at these areas before you make a decision about whether to use it.

The Reformation is a good era to look at to measure a text. If the facts are presented well there the rest of the work is likely to be good. Another test case is the so-called "Black Legend" of early Spanish colonization of the New World. Many texts ignore the good the Spanish did, and the truly high motives of the missionaries, in favor of the wicked practices of some of the Spanish governors, who acted in defiance of the King's orders. American history materials that discuss only the so-called *Enlightenment* as a source of thought for the founding fathers and ignore the legacy of common law and Christianity are suspect. And any text that discusses the Dark Ages as a time of intellectual poverty, ignoring St. Thomas, the University of Paris, St. Bonaventure and St. Albert, doesn't know what it is talking about.

In general, it is Catholicism that suffers at the hands of Protestant or secular history, and it is there that you look in evaluating the usefulness of a given text. This doesn't mean that only texts written by Catholics are any good. Sometimes non-Catholic authors and historians are gifted and accurate in their presentations. *Children of the New Forest* by Captain Frederic Marryat, for example, is an enjoyable fictional history of the time of the Roundheads and Charles II. Captain Marryat is not a Catholic, but his presentation of the Catholics in his book is fair and accurate as far as it goes.

There are specifically Catholic texts, of course. Many of them are out of print. Nevertheless, I have included some of the best on my list of additional or alternative history readings for this grade, because they are worth looking for in used book stores and thrift stores. I have also suggested some books that are in print which we have found to be exceptionally good.

**AMERICAN GOVERNMENT AND ECONOMICS** — *American Government and Economics In Christian Perspective* BY LAUREL HICKS, GEORGE T. THOMPSON, MICHAEL R. LOWMAN AND GEORGE C. COCHRAN (A BEKA) (5), WITH STUDENT TESTS AND REVIEWS AND THE ANSWER KEY (ALSO 5)

This text presents the Constitution of the United States clearly and thoroughly. It gives the student the opportunity to work through the Constitution part by part, seeing each part both in its inception and by discussing the developments that have taken place in the interpretation of those parts. The text discusses the three branches of the government and their constitutional powers. It treats of the abuses of those powers that have occurred. It presents a coherent view of the understanding of government and economics that the founders of our country had. The student tests and reviews may be used for reinforcement and motivation, if they are helpful for your student. This is not a Catholic text, but it is Christian and is written by people with a grasp of their subject.

**LATIN** — *Latin II* BY FT. ROBERT HENLE (20)

*Latin II* continues the study of the Latin language. It thoroughly covers the subjunctive, the sequence of tenses, result and purpose clauses, and the other appropriate concepts. This year is the last year of grammar. Next year the Latin course will concentrate on translation.

**ART/MUSIC** — VARIOUS WORKS IN BOTH CATEGORIES

The student should explore this area on his own, but you might suggest that a review of the periods of music, correlated with art of the same time would make an interesting study.

## Tentative Schedule for Eleventh Grade

| Mon. | Tues. | Wed. | Thurs. | Fri. |
| --- | --- | --- | --- | --- |
| Math | Math | Math | Math | Math |
| English | English | English | English | English |
| Latin | Latin | Latin | Latin | History |
| Religion | Religion | Religion | Religion | |

History reading and writing to be done in the evening or on Friday

# GRADE ELEVEN RESOURCE LISTS

## LIST OF ADDITIONAL OR ALTERNATIVE HISTORY READINGS FOR ELEVENTH GRADE

An "L" after the author's name indicates that the library or used book sources will be your best bet for securing this title, "IP" indicates that the book is currently in print.

## RUSSIAN HISTORY

| | | |
|---|---|---|
| *Peter the Great, His Life and World* | ROBERT K. MASSIE | IP |

## FRENCH HISTORY

| | | |
|---|---|---|
| *Louis and Antoinette* | VINCENT CRONIN | L |
| *Louis XI: The Universal Spider* | PAUL MURRAY KENDALL | IP |
| *Saint Louis* | MARGARET LABARGE | L |
| *To the Scaffold: The Life of Marie Antoinette* | CAROLLY ERICKSON | L |
| *History of the French Revolution* | JULES MICHELET | IP |

## ITALIAN HISTORY

| | | |
|---|---|---|
| *The Borgias* | IVAN CLOULAS | L |
| *The Civilization of the Renaissance* | JACOB BURCKHARDT | IP |

## GENERAL MEDIEVAL

| | | |
|---|---|---|
| *Chronicles of the Crusades* | JOINVILLE AND VILLEHARDOUIN | IP |

# ENGLISH HISTORY

| | | |
|---|---|---|
| *History of the Kings of Britain* | GEOFFREY OF MONMOUTH | IP |
| *Richard the Third:* | | |
|    *The Great Debate* | PAUL MURRAY KENDALL | IP |
| *Queen Elizabeth* | THEODORE MAYNARD | L |
| *Eleanor of Aquitaine and* | | |
|    *the Four Kings* | AMY KELLY | IP |
| *Catherine of Aragon* | GARRETT MATTINGLY | IP |
| *Bloody Mary* | CAROLLY ERICKSON | IP |

# SPANISH HISTORY

| | | |
|---|---|---|
| *The Emperor Charles V* | KARL BRANDI | L |
| *Tree of Hate* | PHILIP WAYNE POWELL | L |
| *Columbus and Cortez,* | | |
|    *Conquerors for Christ* | JOHN EIDSMOE | IP |
| *Isabella of Spain:* | | |
|    *The Catholic Queen* | WARREN CARROLL | IP |
| *Christopher Columbus's* | | |
|    *Book of Prophecies* | KAY BRIGHAM | IP |
| *The Conquest of Granada* | WASHINGTON IRVING | L |
| *The Last Crusader* | LOUIS DE WOHL | L |
| *Cortes of Mexico* | RONALD SYME | L |
| *California Missions* | | |
|    (A PICTORIAL HISTORY) | SUNSET PUBLISHING CORP. | IP |
| *Junipero Serra* | DON DENEVI | L |

# Twelfth Grade Curriculum

**Sources for items followed by a number in parentheses may be found at the back of the book under the suppliers list.**

## RELIGION — RELIGION 12 (20)

The text for this course, *Following Christ in the World* is written by Dr. Anne Carroll and is only available from Seton. It covers many timely issues and practical considerations from a Catholic viewpoint. There are references to the encyclicals of the Church and to the magisterial teaching of the Church. This course reviews topics covered in earlier classes, such as the immortality of the soul and the divinity of Christ. It also introduces new material that all Catholics should be familiar with, such as liberal capitalism and the social encyclicals, war and peace, and justice in the marketplace. It contains a small section of philosophical terms and concepts that whets the student's appetite for more.

## MATHEMATICS — *Pre-Calculus* (20)

This course is a preparation for a college calculus course. It covers intermediate algebra, analytic geometry, trigonometry, and circular, polynomial, and transcendental functions. Seton offers the text, *Pre-Calculus Mathematics*, with the teacher's guide and solutions manual.

If your child is going to college it is important to continue with some kind of mathematics through high school. College level mathematics courses will be much easier and less time consuming if the algebraic skills acquired earlier are not forgotten. Additionally, this is where mathematics gets interesting.

## ENGLISH — *English 12* (20)

*The Prose and Poetry of England,* an out of print Catholic book, is the text for this course. The analysis expected of the student is consonant with his abilities at this level. In other words, the work expected of the student is more difficult than in previous courses, but not more difficult than he can handle. It requires more subtlety, a more discriminating interpretation of texts, and an attention to language. These are the skills that this stage of education should be directed to.

HISTORY — *A History of Medieval Spain* BY JOSEPH O'CALLAGHAN (1,7) OR *Philip II, Isabella of Spain, Characters of the Inquisition, Saint Teresa of Avila,* ALL BY WILLIAM THOMAS WALSH (14)

Continue with the study begun last year. This year, however, assign a number of papers. Let your student pick the topics, but you suggest the mode of the paper. The ninth grade history curriculum includes some writing suggestions that would work here. Such suggestions include first person descriptions of the time read about as though you were living at the time, the pros and cons of a particular question, the imagined recorded conversation between two important characters from history, and narrative essays. Four papers, each a minimum of 2,500 words, will provide the final writing exercise of your child's classical curriculum. I think you and your child will find that the ease with which such a project may be undertaken and completed is a sign that you have both succeeded in your educational goals.

LATIN — *Latin III* BY FR. ROBERT HENLE (20)

*Latin III* is designed to use the grammatical knowledge that your child has gained up to this point. It contains exercises and translations based mainly on Cicero. Following, as it does, years of Latin classes, it is quite easy to do, and it is a pleasure because the student sees how much he has learned, and how useful it is.

ART/MUSIC — VARIOUS WORKS IN BOTH CATEGORIES

Encourage your child to continue to listen to good music. Arrange to go to a concert or two during the year with him. It is important that he continue his acquaintance with classical music now, because as he moves away from home he will be bombarded with the modern ugly alternatives.

If you have art museums near you plan a few trips this year. While there isn't the same level of exposure to unattractive art as there is to such music in our society, the love of great art is such a pleasure in itself that you want to encourage it in your child as long as you are able to do so.

## TENTATIVE SCHEDULE FOR TWELFTH GRADE

| Mon. | Tues. | Wed. | Thurs. | Fri. |
|------|-------|------|--------|------|
| Math | Math | Math | Math | Math |
| English | English | English | English | English |
| Latin | Latin | Latin | Latin | History |
| Religion | Religion | Religion | Religion | |

HISTORY READING AND WRITING TO BE DONE IN THE EVENING OR ON FRIDAY

# NOTES

# A Final Word

---

"Is the trivium, then, a sufficient education for life? Properly taught, I believe that it should be. At the end of the Dialectic, the children will probably seem to be far behind their coevals brought up on old-fashioned 'modern' methods, so far as detailed knowledge of specific subjects is concerned. But after the age of 14 they should be able to overhaul the others hand over fist. Indeed, I am not at all sure that a pupil thoroughly proficient in the Trivium would not be fit to proceed immediately to the university at the age of 16, thus proving himself the equal of his medieval counterpart ..."

— Dorothy Leigh Sayers

# Suppliers

1) CHECK ANY GOOD BOOKSTORE.
IF IT IS NOT IN STOCK THEY
CAN ORDER IT.

2) CHECK AN EDUCATIONAL SUPPLY STORE.

3) THE ALWAYS INCOMPLETE CATALOG
LIFETIME BOOKS AND GIFTS
3900 CHALET SUZANNE DRIVE
LAKE WALES, FL 33853
(800) 377-0390

4) STELLA MARIS BOOKS
P.O. BOX 11483
FORT WORTH, TX 76110
(800) 772-5928

5) A BEKA CATALOG
A BEKA BOOK
BOX 1800
PENSACOLA, FL 32523-9160
(800) 874-2352

6) ST. MICHAEL'S
4525 GARFIELD AVE.
CARMICHAEL, CA 95608
(916) 486-4961

7) USED BOOK STORES

8) GREENLEAF PRESS
1570 OLD LA GUARDO ROAD
LEBANON, TN 37087
(615) 449-1617

9) BETHLEHEM BOOKS
R.R. # 1 BOX 137-A
MINTO, ND 58261
(701) 248-3866

10) TOWN BOOK FAIRS
    1331 RED CEDAR CIRCLE
    FORT COLLINS, CO 80524
    (303) 493-6311
    *Send $2.00 for catalogue*

11) CANON PRESS
    P.O. Box 8741
    Moscow, ID 83843
    (800) 488-2034

12) OUR LADY OF VICTORY
    4436 ALPINE
    POST FALLS, ID 83854
    (208) 773-7265

13) INSECT LORE
    P.O. Box 1535
    SHAFTER, CA 93263
    (800) LIVE BUG

14) TAN BOOK PUBLISHERS
    P.O. Box 424
    ROCKFORD, IL 61105
    (800) 437-5876

15) TIMBERDOODLE
    E. 1510 SPENCER LAKE RD.
    SHELTON, WA 98584
    (206) 426-0672

16) LONGMAN PRESS
    10 BANK STREET
    WHITE PLAINS, NY 10606-1951
    (800) 447-2226
    — FOR TEACHER'S EDITIONS YOU WILL NEED TO ORDER
      THROUGH A SCHOOL THAT WILL COOPERATE WITH YOU.

17) CONSERVATIVE BOOK CLUB
    33 OAKLAND AVE.
    HARRISON, NY 10528-3739

18) CHRISTIAN TEACHING MATERIALS
    14275 ELM AVE.
    P.O. Box 639
    GLENPOOL, OK 74033-0639
    (918) 322-3420

19) WARRINER'S GRAMMAR
   PUBLISHED BY:
   HARCOURT-BRACE JOVANOVICH PUBLISHERS
   6277 SEA HARBOR DR.
   ORLANDO, FL 32821
   (707) 763-1000 (WESTERN DIVISION)
   (201) 368-2200 (EASTERN DIVISION)
   — FOR TEACHER'S EDITIONS YOU WILL NEED TO ORDER
     THROUGH A SCHOOL THAT WILL COOPERATE WITH YOU.

20) SETON HOME STUDY SCHOOL
   1350 PROGRESS DR.
   P.O. BOX 396
   FRONT ROYAL, VA 22630
   (703) 636-9990

21) EDUCATORS PUBLISHING SERVICE, INC.
   31 SMITH PLACE
   CAMBRIDGE, MA 02138-1000
   (800) 225-5750

22) HAYES SCHOOL PUBLISHERS, INC.
   321 PENNWOOD AVE.
   PITTSBURGH, PA 15221-3389
   (800) 245-6234

23) THE MOORE FOUNDATION
   BOX 1
   CAMAS, WA 98607
   (206) 853-2736

24) THE CATHOLIC HOME EDUCATOR
   P.O. BOX 420225
   SAN DIEGO, CA 92142

25) MOTHER OF DIVINE GRACE INDEPENDENT STUDY PROGRAM
   P.O. BOX 1440
   OJAI, CA 93023
   (805) 646-5818
   — MODG CARRIES *Concepts and Challenges in Science,* FR. HENLE'S
     LATIN BOOKS AND KEYS, AND IS ABLE TO ORDER TEACHER
     EDITIONS FROM LONGMAN PRESS AND HARCOURT BRACE
     JOVANOVICH.